Cape May

THE INFORMED TRAVELER'S GUIDE

Cape May

Russell Roberts

THE INFORMED TRAVELER'S GUIDE

STACKPOLE
BOOKS

Published by
STACKPOLE BOOKS
5067 Ritter Road
Mechanicsburg, PA 17055
www.stackpolebooks.com

Printed in China

10 9 8 7 6 5 4 3 2 1

FIRST EDITION

Design by Beth Oberholtzer
Cover design by Wendy Reynolds

Cover: Emlen Physick Estate. MID-ATLANTIC CENTER FOR THE ARTS

Library of Congress Cataloging-in-Publication Data

Roberts, Russell, 1953–
    Cape May / Russell Roberts. – 1st ed.
        p.   cm. – (Informed traveler's guide)
    Includes index.
    ISBN-13: 978-0-8117-3375-5 (pbk.)
    ISBN-10: 0-8117-3375-0 (pbk.)
    1. Cape May (N.J.)–Guidebooks.   2. Cape May Region (N.J.)–Guidebooks.
I. Title.

F144.C23R63   2008
917.49'980444–dc22

2007018727

CONTENTS

Introduction

If Cape May were a highway billboard, it would read something like this: "National Historic Landmark Town. Victorian Architecture. Bed-and-Breakfast Capital of America." The words would be accompanied by a picture of an easily recognizable Victorian-era building, with peaks, gingerbread, and a spacious front porch. As billboards are supposed to do, it would form a snapshot in your mind as you whizzed by it on the highway, and you'd feel you knew the whole Cape May story. If the car held just you and your spouse, and you liked Victorian-oriented things, you'd smile and nod at each other, thinking of bed-and-breakfasts, doilies on the furniture, rocking chairs, and afternoon teas on big front porches.

Kids, who can sniff out a boring vacation trip faster than they can spend money (well, *almost* as fast), would roll their eyes in despair at the sight of that billboard and frantically begin thinking of the names of distant relatives with whom they could stay so they wouldn't have to go there. They'd look at each other and grimace, thinking of stuffy old houses and being told don't touch this, don't sit on that. Boring, boring, boring!

That's Cape May, right? Sedate, historical, beautiful, romantic, yet boring for kids.

Actually, nothing could be further from the truth.

True, the atmosphere of Cape May is most definitely sedate and tranquil, unlike the frantic whirl of other coastal resort towns. Time and calendar tend not to matter in Cape May. The whole Victorian atmosphere, with tree-lined streets complete with horse-drawn carriages, gives the impression of a yesteryear, a place where the impatient chirping of a cell phone and clipped business conversations are as out of place as tomato sauce on ice cream.

And it certainly is historic. Victorian-era architecture is all around you in Cape May. You can't go very far without running into a historic building or edifice. Indeed, there's so much history here that the whole town has been declared a national historic landmark.

As far as being beautiful, in Cape May you can walk down shady streets while flowers of every color pop out at you from lovely, manicured gardens. You can watch a fiery sun slowly rise over the misty morning ocean and throw a thousand sparkling fingers over the water's surface. You can walk across a sandy beach and listen for the gentle call of a heron.

But boring? Nothing could be further from the truth.

Like an onion, Cape May has many different layers. If you look beneath the Victorian architecture, B&B lodging, and slower pace, you'll find funky shops, fun family dining, boardwalk amusements, fascinating activities, and enough tours and special events to provide something of interest for every visitor. And of course, there's the beach.

Although Cape May's genteel atmosphere appeals to adults, the town also has plenty to offer for the whole family. CONGRESS HALL

So there's more to Cape May than initially meets the eye. That's where this book comes in. It's here to help you discover the many facets of Cape May.

Much more so than with most vacation destinations, Cape May's present is inexorably tied to its past. A knowledge of the city's history will help you understand the town better.

Philadelphia has given us many things, such as Benjamin Franklin, Independence Hall, and cheesesteaks. It has also given us Cape May.

By 1790, with a population of 42,000, Philadelphia was the largest city in the young United States of America and had the busiest seaport. Ships heading into Philadelphia via the Delaware River had to round the southernmost tip of New Jersey, and those leaving the City of Brotherly Love for the Atlantic Ocean and then to the ports of New York, Boston, or Charleston also had to cruise past this point.

Right at the very end of New Jersey was the village of Cape Island, as Cape May was known through the eighteenth and early nineteenth centuries. Henry Hudson had initially discovered the area in 1609. In 1620, Dutch captain Cornelius Jacobsen Mey explored New Jersey and the Delaware Bay area. Suitably impressed, he declared the region's climate as good as that in his homeland of Holland and named Cape Mey after himself. (Sometime over the next century, Mey was anglicized to May.) Since then, the region's gentle ocean and white sand beaches had attracted just a smattering of people. But with all those people now coming and going to and from Philadelphia and passing Cape Island in the process, how long would it remain a hidden jewel?

Soon people began coming to Cape May to enjoy the air and water. The footsteps of these first tourists have been covered by the sands of time, but a 1766 real estate ad in the *Pennsylvania Gazette* talks about the land being located "in the Lower Precinct of the County of Cape May, and within One Mile and a Half of the Sea Shore; where a Number resort for health, and bathing in the Water." By the beginning of the nineteenth century, Cape May was well established as a destination.

For a long time, the principal means of getting to Cape May was by boat. Sailing sloops began regular trips to the area in the first few years of the nineteenth century. Steamboats followed around 1816. The alternative method was to journey there by "jersey wagon," a bone-jarring trip in a no-frills freight wagon that was akin to having someone repeatedly bash your spine with a hammer—with you paying for the privilege.

As more and more people arrived in the area, hotels, inns, and boardinghouses began popping up. In 1816, a huge three-story structure called the Big House opened, with the capacity to accommodate 100 guests. In 1828, it was called Congress Hall—the same name it has today as one of the city's most distinctive hotels.

Visitors to Congress Hall and other lodging houses came to the seashore to enjoy sea-bathing, which was a far cry from our modern swimming. The bather would wade out into the water, vigorously jump up and down like someone who has just stepped on a sharp shell, and then return to the beach. Numerous medical benefits were attributed to sea-bathing, including stimulation of the circulatory system. For women, whose typical bathing attire contained more than ten yards of flannel, modesty being more important than comfort in those days, sea-bathing must indeed have stimulated the circulatory system—to the point of desperately trying not to be dragged under the water and drowned by their heavy wet clothes.

Congress Hall, one of the first lodging houses in Cape May, has been a favorite of many famous visitors.
CONGRESS HALL

In August 1847, Cape May had its first celebrity visitor when famous politician Henry Clay, "the Great Compromiser," visited the resort. Even though it was toward the tail end of the season, the town's hotels filled up once again, and various dignitaries arrived to see the famous man in the flesh. Clay had gone to the resort to quietly grieve over the death of his son in the Mexican War. Suddenly he found himself besieged by his fans. His attempts to take relaxing sea baths were foiled by frenzied females who pursued him with scissors, trying to cut a lock of his hair for a souvenir. Eventually Clay returned to Washington, undoubtedly with much shorter hair.

Despite local legend about another famous visitor, a Mr. A. Lincoln who visited in July 1849 is thought not to have been *that* A. Lincoln. It seems likely that this was instead a Philadelphia grocer named Abel Lincoln.

As Cape May rolled into the 1850s, it was unchallenged as America's most famous seashore resort. This was further reinforced by the beginning of construction in 1852 of the massive Mount Vernon Hotel, reputedly the largest seaside hotel in the world. But a massive fire on September 5, 1856, destroyed the hotel and seemed an omen of future bad times.

The construction of a railroad from Camden, New Jersey, in 1854 to a tiny coastal town called Atlantic City was about to radically alter the destination plans of everyone heading to the Jersey Shore. Even more significantly, the growing tensions between the country's North and South, which were about to erupt into civil

war, spelled the end of Cape May's Southern clientele. As it is located below the Mason-Dixon Line, it had been getting a large number of visitors from the South. Virtually overnight, a group that had been pumping $50,000 annually into the local economy vanished from Cape May, never to return. The town's hustle and bustle slowed to a crawl.

Hotels fell into disrepair, as no money was available to fix them. Inns that once had been filled to capacity now had more ghosts than people. The *New York Herald Tribune* wrote a story about the "paintless, graceless, and comfortless hotels" in Cape May (putting the lie to the notion that no publicity is ever bad publicity).

But the wolf was thwarted right at the door in the mid-1860s, when the railroad finally arrived in Cape May. New money flowed into the resort, and some of it began going toward a completely new venture: the construction of summer vacation cottages. Even a devastating fire in 1869 could not stall the resort's rebirth.

Cape May experienced its ups and downs over the next few years, until another huge fire in 1878. This one burned about thirty-five acres, along with seven hotels, more than thirty cottages and boardinghouses, and about 2,000 bathhouses. But this time the town rebuilt in a smaller, more intimate fashion. Magnificent new cottages were again constructed, but not at the previous pace. As the twentieth century dawned, the town seemed to be in a holding pattern.

Nothing signified a resort at the crossroads as much as the Hotel Cape May project. Part of an ambitious and grandiose development scheme, the opulent multistory hotel was going to be the cornerstone of a "new" Cape May. Auto pioneers Louis Chevrolet and Henry Ford even staged auto races on the beach in front of where the hotel was being built to generate publicity. When the hotel opened in

Cape May has avoided large-scale development, allowing the town to retain its serene character.

the spring of 1908, the ceremonies included the governor of New Jersey. Cape May, it was assured, was on its way.

Six months later, however, it turned out that the town was on its way to nowhere when the Hotel Cape May abruptly closed. (The building was later used as a military hospital during World War I and a Naval Annex house during World War II.)

But the old saying about every dark cloud having a silver lining was never truer than in the collapse of this real estate project. The aim of the developers had been to tear down many old, quaint, and supposedly outdated buildings in Cape May, replacing them with modern brick and steel structures in an effort to mimic Atlantic City. If the project had succeeded, the current Cape May would be very different than it is today.

The rest of the shore was rapidly being developed during the early twentieth century, with new resort towns popping up all along the New Jersey coast. Vacationers had numerous destinations to choose from. Stuck all the way at the bottom of New Jersey, Cape May seemed like a distant echo of the past.

Perhaps the town's status was best summed up by what happened to the concrete ship *Atlantus* in 1926. A dozen such ships had been built during World War I because of a steel shortage, until it was realized that maneuvering them was like maneuvering . . . well, a concrete block. One of the ships was purchased by a Baltimore man, who planned to use it as part of a dock for a proposed ferry between Cape May and Cape Henlopen, Delaware.

The ship was towed to Cape May, concrete ships not being particularly speedy or seaworthy, and readied for being sunk as part of the dock. But during a bad storm, *Atlantus* broke away from her mooring and took a nosedive directly into the sandy bottom of Delaware Bay, never to be moved again. Although much of the ship was visible at first, today just a tiny piece can be seen above water, as she settles farther and farther into the sand with each passing year. Like the ship, Cape May remained a town stuck in the mud as the years rolled on by.

In the mid-1950s, a new superhighway called the Garden State Parkway was completed along the coast of New Jersey. Suddenly all the shore resort towns in the state were easily accessible. Cape May, at the very bottom of the Parkway, seemed a relic of yesteryear. With no new development, the town remained locked in the past. "They do not do much tearing down in Cape May," noted a Philadelphia newspaper.

But what no one realized then was that this was going to be Cape May's salvation.

Some residents were already saying that the town needed to capitalize on its history, as reflected in its many Victorian buildings. This idea gained emphasis after the devastation of the March 1962 northeaster, one of the most terrible storms ever to strike the entire Jersey Shore. Cape May was faced with a choice: either rebuild with modern buildings or capitalize on its existing old-style architecture.

The move for Cape May to emphasize its past was further reinforced by a report stating that the city "was sitting on a goldmine" with "the most complete . . . grouping of mid-nineteenth century buildings east of the Mississippi." The idea for the town to save its older buildings gained momentum, but there were still some notable exceptions. For example, when the entire city of Cape May was listed on the federal National Register of Historic Places in 1970, the designation had to be sneaked past certain city officials, who were afraid it would damage their efforts to secure urban renewal project funding for the city. Thankfully, it did. In fact, one of these officials even tried to get the Historic Register designation overturned.

Cape May's Victorian character is a big draw for modern-day visitors. MID-ATLANTIC CENTER FOR THE ARTS

People in Victorian dress wander the streets, enhancing the feeling that time has stopped in Cape May. MID-ATLANTIC CENTER FOR THE ARTS

But once the Emlen Physick Estate became the first Victorian building restored in town and people realized what the town's future would be like with dozens of restored Victorian-era buildings, there was no holding back. Sleepy Cape May became stylish Cape May, the bed-and-breakfast capital of the East Coast.

Today the past is the present—and the future—of Cape May. Few people who visit the resort and marvel at the Victorian architecture realize how close it all came to being bulldozed for soulless buildings of glass and steel. Even fewer realize that they are visiting one of America's oldest seaside resorts.

GETTING TO CAPE MAY

Cape May is probably the easiest resort in the world to reach by car. The city sits at the tip of southern New Jersey and at the very end of the Garden State Parkway. When you run out of Parkway, you've run out of New Jersey and reached Cape May. Conversely, if you're coming from anywhere in the South, Cape May is the very first piece of New Jersey that you hit.

For folks who find those directions just a tad nonspecific, here's some more detailed information:

By Car

After Getting off the Cape May–Lewes Ferry:

Take Sandman Boulevard (Route 9) to 109 south, cross the Cape May Bridge (no toll), and remain straight on Lafayette.

From Atlantic City:

Take the Atlantic City Expressway west to the Garden State Parkway south to Route 109 south, then continue as above.

From Philadelphia:

Cross the Walt Whitman Bridge to Route 42 south to the Atlantic City Expressway east to the Garden State Parkway south to Route 109 south, and then continue as above. Or follow Route 42 south to Route 55 south to Route 347 south to Garden State Parkway south to Route 109 south.

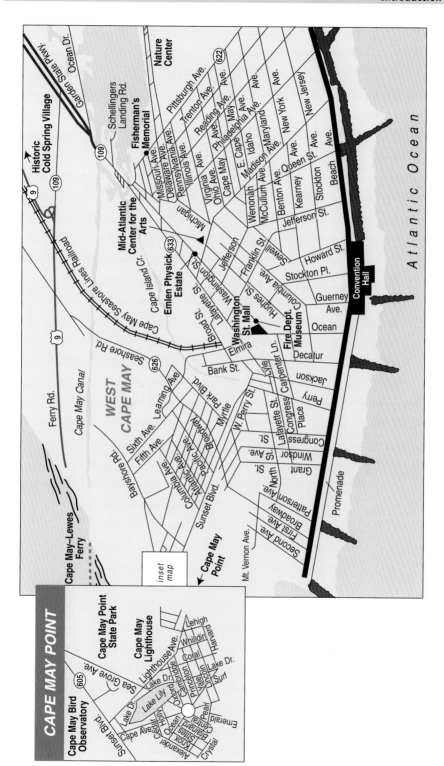

From Washington, D.C.:

Take I-95 north to the Delaware Memorial Bridge to Route 55 south to Route 347 south to the Garden State Parkway south to Route 109 south, then continue as above.

From New York City:

Take I-95 south (New Jersey Turnpike) to the Garden State Parkway south to Route 109 South, then continue as above.

From Quebec:

Take Route 40 to Route 15 to I-87 (New York Thruway) to the Garden State Parkway south to Route 109 south, then continue as above.

From Toronto:

Take Queen Elizabeth Way to I-90 to I-81 to the Pennsylvania Turnpike Northeast Extension (I-476) south to the Schuylkill Expressway (Route 76) east. Then follow the directions for Philadelphia.

Heading north on Route 109: Turn left onto Seashore Road (fourth light), which becomes Broadway. At the traffic light, make a left onto Sunset Road/West Perry. This brings you to Lafayette Street.

By Air

The Atlantic City International Airport, Civil Terminal Suite 106, Egg Harbor Township, NJ 08234 (609-645-7895, 888-235-9229, www.acairport.com), serves all of southern New Jersey and is the closest airport to Cape May. From here it takes about forty minutes to reach the town. Access the airport by taking the Atlantic City Expressway to Exit 9. Carriers include Spirit Airlines (800-772-7117) and Delta (800-221-1212), but with the way airlines are going, it's best to check with the airport or your carrier.

By Bus

New Jersey Transit (973-762-5100, 800-772-2222, www.njtransit.com) offers regularly scheduled bus service to Cape May from Philadelphia and Atlantic City. Other stops include North Cape May, Villas, and Rio Grande.

By Ferry

The Cape May–Lewes Ferry (800-643-3779) will carry you and your car between Cape May and Lewes, Delaware. See the listing in chapter 1 for complete information.

ENTERING CAPE MAY

Normally entering a town is no big deal. But entering Cape May from the Garden State Parkway requires a bit of awareness, or you'll find yourself heading right back out of town!

Once you leave the Parkway, turn left at the traffic light and stay in the right lane. You're now on Route 109 south. Once you go over the large bridge, you'll be in the outskirts of Cape May. Here's where it gets tricky.

Your road now becomes one-way. To go to the beach area and drive along Beach Drive, you must immediately get into the left lane. You'll then be forced to take another left, which quickly ends at a T in front of a series of billboards. Go left. This will then turn into Pittsburgh Avenue. Go straight on Pittsburgh for about three-fourths of a mile, and you'll come to Beach Drive. Go right (left takes you out of town along Beach Drive). You'll be driving alongside the beach and ocean. Shortly you'll come to the Promenade, motels, and turnoffs to the right to get to the Historic District or the center of town.

If you prefer to go to downtown Cape May first, perhaps to do a little shopping at the Washington Street Mall, then when your road becomes one-way upon entering town, get immediately in the right lane and go straight. This is Lafayette Street, which will shortly become two-way. Follow this for about one mile, until you reach the traffic light next to the Acme supermarket parking lot. Turn left at this light and you're now on Ocean Street at the Washington Street Mall. Go straight along Ocean, past the mall, to reach Columbia Avenue and the other streets of the Historic District. If you continue straight through the light by the Acme instead of turning left, you'll be heading into Cape May Point and West Cape May.

LEAVING CAPE MAY

Leaving Cape May is considerably easier than entering it. Following Washington Street straight will bring you back to the connection for the Garden State Parkway. Taking Beach Drive to Pittsburgh Avenue will also connect you to the Parkway. Follow the signs for the Parkway and you can't go wrong.

THINGS YOU MUST KNOW ABOUT CAPE MAY

Within the four square miles of Cape May Island are four municipalities: Cape May, Cape May Point, Lower Township, and West Cape May. Cape May itself has so much to see and do that your daily planner will quickly run out of room. But there are excellent attractions scattered about in the other municipalities as well, so don't hesitate to explore.

Cape May transforms into West Cape May around Swain's hardware store. A dry town, West Cape May has its own distinct list of activities, festivals, and the like, topped off by the inimitable Lima Bean Festival. North Cape May, another town name you'll encounter in this book, begins over the West Cape May Bridge.

Cape May is best seen by walking. Driving in Cape May, particularly in the summer, is an experience rivaled only by root canals and political speeches. In addition, you'll be feeding parking meters so often that they'll become like part of the family. Another good way to see Cape May is by bicycle. The town is small, the streets interconnect, and the traffic usually moves slowly enough. There are several places that rent bicycles, and many hotels and guest houses provide them for their guests.

The long road running parallel to the ocean is called, alternatively, Beach Drive or Beach Avenue. So do not be confused; these refer to the same street.

The Cape May Post Office is on Washington Street, near the end toward Ocean Street and the pedestrian mall. The area code for a great majority of Cape May is 609. Some places use the new area code, 856, but try 609 first.

It's important to plan ahead, no matter when you plan to visit. Cape May is a year-round destination. Unlike most of the rest of the Jersey Shore, which begins a slow slide into slumber after Labor Day, Cape May keeps chugging along. Mid-September through October, and even into early November, is an extremely popular time in Cape May. Accommodations are often easier to obtain, rates are lower, the town is more deserted, and the weather is usually still fairly warm and comfortable. The town schedules numerous popular special events during these months.

Christmas season starts right around Thanksgiving and is one of the most wondrous times of the year in town. As far as crowds, think summer with coats. It can get that crazy, crowded, and busy. After the calendar page turns to another year, Valentine's Day and Presidents' Day mark the unofficial start of the upcoming season. So really, January is about the only "dead time" at Cape May. But some people enjoy coming to Cape May at that time of year, as the restaurants and inns that are open are far less crowded, so you will find visitors even then.

Therefore, you should not head down to Cape May thinking that you can just slide into a specific hotel or B&B. Reservations are always a good idea. But having said that, it's always possible to go down to Cape May on a whim and have a very nice time. Contradictory advice? Not really. If you have your heart set on a *specific* B&B, hotel, tour, or restaurant, then, yes, reservations are important in a town where people often book the same weekend a year in advance. But Cape May has so many fine accommodations that even if you go down on the spur of the moment, you will almost certainly be able to find something.

Hours of operation for stores and restaurants vary depending on the time of year. As one store owner said about business hours in colder weather, "After Christmas, I may open on the weekends if the weather's nice." So be forewarned: Call first before you head down in the off-season, to make sure the places you want to visit are going to be open.

Innkeepers and hotel proprietors tend to look askance at personal checks. They may take them, but they often require them far in advance so that they can clear first. This is a major resort area, with visitors from all over the world.

Opportunities for smoking are limited. There are several reasons for this. One is that New Jersey has a very restrictive smoking law, which says that you can't smoke in a public building in the state, except in the Atlantic City casinos (and at this writing, that exception was being reviewed). Another reason is that these are old buildings, and one careless cigarette butt can start a devastating fire. At most, you may be allowed to smoke on an establishment's open-air porch. But many inns, restaurants, and hotels are now smoke-free, period.

In New Jersey, free beaches are few and far between. To use the Cape May beaches, beach tags are required for adults and children age twelve and over from Memorial Day weekend until mid-September to late September.

RESOURCES

Cape May County Chamber of Commerce
13 Crest Haven Rd.
P.O. Box 74
Cape May Court House, NJ 08210
Telephone: 609-465-7181
Fax: 609-465-5017
Website: www.cmccofc.com
The Chamber's Information Center (Garden State Parkway Exit 11) is open 9 to 5 daily from mid-April to mid-October and Monday through Friday from mid-October to mid-April.

Cape May County Department of Tourism
4 Moore Rd.
Cape May Court House, NJ 08210
Telephone: 609-463-6415 or 800-227-2297
Fax: 609-465-4639
Website: www.thejerseycape.net
The department will provide information on the entire Jersey Cape and, on request, send a vacation-planning kit.

Chamber of Commerce of Greater Cape May
609 Lafayette St., 2nd Floor
P.O. Box 556
Cape May, NJ 08204
Telephone: 609-884-5508
Fax: 609-884-2054
Website: www.capemaychamber.com

Cape May Welcome & Information Center
405 Lafayette St.
Cape May, NJ 08204
Telephone: 609-884-9562
Located at Garden State Parkway mile marker 18.
This full-service visitors center is located in the Ocean View Service Arena, and run by the NJ Division of Travel and Tourism. It has maps, brochures, and other information. It is open 9 to 5 daily, year-round.

Mid-Atlantic Center for the Arts
Emlen Physick Estate
1048 Washington St.
P.O. Box 340
Cape May, NJ 08204
Telephone: 609-884-5404 or 800-275-4278
Fax: 609-884-2006
Website: www.capemaymac.org

Mid-Atlantic Center for the Arts

If you hear people in Cape May say, "MAC," they're not asking for directions to a fast-food restaurant. Rather, they are referring to the Mid-Atlantic Center for the Arts, known as MAC and one of the main providers of unique Cape May tours and other visitor services.

MAC was founded in September 1970, at a critical juncture in Cape May's history. The town was in the midst of a pitched battle between the city government, which wanted to tear down and build anew, and historic preservationists, who wanted to start tapping into the city's wealth of Victorian buildings. It all came together in the form of the abandoned Emlen Physick Estate, which at that time was so dilapidated it would have given the term "haunted house" a bad name. When plans were announced to raze this historic home to make room for tract housing, the battle was on.

The city government refused to accept a federal grant to restore the estate, citing a loss of tax ratables, and MAC's leaders subsequently won at the ballot box in November to get the historic preservation ball rolling. The federal grant was accepted by the new administration, and MAC was off and running.

MAC's first priority was to restore the Physick Estate. Today it remains the town's only Victorian house museum. But MAC didn't stop there. Early in the game, it launched the first guided walking tour of Cape May, then followed this up with a trolley tour of historic homes. As Cape May grew in popularity, MAC responded with a growing number of offerings and special events. The four-day Victorian Weekend expanded into a ten-day Victorian Week, Christmas Candlelight House Tours became a Christmas season full of activities, and Music Festivals, Sherlock Holmes Weekends, and other special events joined MAC's ever-growing roster.

Today MAC is as synonymous with Cape May as Victorian architecture, and just as pervasive, and it is the wise visitor who checks out what weekly activities and events MAC is offering. From its humble beginnings, MAC has evolved into a multifaceted, nonprofit cultural organization that promotes the preservation and interpretation of Cape May's Victorian heritage and the performing arts with a year-round schedule of special events and tours. Membership in MAC is open to all and provides free admission to certain attractions and tours, as well as other benefits such as a discount at the various museum shops it operates in the region.

TRANSPORTATION

Although Cape May is best seen on foot or by bicycle, there are other options.

Trolley

The Five Mile Beach Electric Railway (not to be confused with the MAC Trolley) will take you around greater Cape May in an open-air trolley car. Call 609-884-5230 for schedule.

Taxis

Several taxi companies operate in Cape May: Aart's Cape May Taxi, 609-898-7433; Carribean Cab Company, 609-523-8000; and High Roller, 609-425-5819, which will take you anywhere around Cape May for $6 per ride.

HEALTH AND SAFETY

Medical
Burdette Tomlin Memorial Hospital
Stone Harbor Blvd. at Rt. 9
(Garden State Parkway Exit 10)
Cape May Court House, NJ 08210
Main number: 609-463-2000
Emergency number: 609-463-2130

Police
643 Washington St.
Cape May, NJ 08204
609-884-9500

Fire Department
Cape May, NJ 08204
609-884-9500

Attractions

Once you've arrived in Cape May, you'll discover a wealth of attractions for a variety of interests. You can bird-watch, see hundreds of zoo animals in natural settings, or look for otters, turtles, and other forms of wildlife. You can swim in the ocean, sunbathe on the beach, search for Cape May "diamonds," or get a bird's-eye view of the blue-green Atlantic. You can visit a home renovated by professional designers, take a historic tour of the "mother" of all Cape May Victorian structures, or ride in a horse-drawn carriage. You can also honor military members lost in service of their country, view the remains of a concrete battleship, or remember fishermen lost at sea. There's something for everyone in Cape May!

THE BEACHES

The beaches at Cape May offer a multitude of activities, depending on what beach you happen to be visiting.

Cape May's Atlantic Ocean beach stretches over two miles along Beach Drive. Even though Cape May is the Victorian Jewel of the East Coast, drawing thousands of people to gaze at its architectural splendor, the town is still a Jersey Shore seaside resort, and its beach is one of its main tourist magnets.

The Cape May beach is at once both similar and dissimilar to other New Jersey Atlantic Ocean beaches. It is not a beach where volleyballs and Frisbees are tossed around, like Point Pleasant or Belmar. It is also not a beach where the aromas of caramel corn and pizza, the screaming of thrill-ride patrons, and the electronic beep of video arcades waft over the summer sand.

Rather, like the town itself, the Cape May beach is more sedate. People sit in beach chairs under large umbrellas and read, or lie on the sand to catch a blessed few extra minutes of sleep.

Charter boats, mainly carrying tour groups, cruise by well offshore. Sometimes dolphins or porpoises, drawn by the familiar sound of the boat's engine or the captain's voice on the loudspeaker, pop up in the boat's wake, eager to greet an old friend. The ocean is often dotted with sailboats, their colorful sails a striking contrast against the blue-green water. Occasionally a small powerboat races by, pulling a person parasailing behind it. Parasailing, with its participants floating by in the sky borne by billowy cloudlike parachutes, is a popular pastime in season at Cape May. Surfing is also allowed at two of the beaches.

Lifeguards are on duty from 10 A.M. to 5 P.M. After 5, when most bathers and sun worshippers are packing up to go home, the surf fishers arrive, and the beach is dotted with poles stuck into holders in the sand, with their lines extending into the water. The town does not like people to remain on the beach after 5:30 P.M.

The calm before the storm: Cape May's beach in early morning, before the summer crowds arrive.
PAT KING-ROBERTS

In New Jersey, just a handful of beaches up and down the entire coastline are free, and all Atlantic Ocean Cape May beachgoers are required to wear a beach badge or beach tag. You might hate them, as most locals and visitors do, but you need them. People do check for them, and woe to the sunbather who does not have one. The tags are sold at various locations in Cape May, including Convention Hall on the weekends, the Information Booth on the Washington Street Mall, and the City Hall information desk at 9643 Washington Street.

Many accommodations offer such amenities as free beach chairs and beach towels. For special-needs guests, Cape May provides free beach wheelchairs. If one is necessary, talk to any lifeguard and a chair will be delivered. You can also get a beach wheelchair from the Beach Patrol by calling (609) 884-9520.

Some Jersey Shore towns have specific names for their beaches because they are privately owned, but Cape May's beaches have informal names generally based on location. Cape May's Atlantic Ocean beach is technically all one beach, and a single badge grants you access to the whole thing. But certain sections of beach are known by specific names, and knowing where they're located can be convenient for the visitor.

Some beach names refer to cross streets off of Beach Drive, such as Broadway Beach, Colonial Beach, Grant Avenue Beach, Jefferson Beach, Philadelphia Beach,

The end of a great Cape May day means the beginning of a great night. MID-ATLANTIC CENTER FOR THE ARTS

Queen Street Beach, and Windsor Avenue Beach. Both Colonial and Jefferson Beaches allow surfing. Congress Hall Beach and Convention Hall Beach are known for their proximity to local landmarks. Two other beaches have acquired names without any geographic significance. Poverty Beach is roughly the last section of the Cape May beach before it ends at the inlet, and Stegers Beach is roughly in the center of Beach Drive, in the vicinity of Uncle Billy's Pancake House.

One thing unique about Cape May is that while relaxing on the beach, you can gaze at stunningly beautiful examples of Victorian architecture. Be it the famous Congress Hall hotel, with its trademark white pillars, or a smaller restaurant, B&B, or home with gingerbread molding and a mansard roof, Victoriana is never far away. It makes for a nice visual, whether you're on the beach or strolling along the Promenade.

What is the Promenade? That's the name of the strip of black asphalt that runs about a mile and a half parallel to the beach and serves as Cape May's boardwalk. Interestingly, there is some evidence that Cape May might have had a boardwalk of actual wood called a "flirtation walk" a few years before Atlantic City invented the boardwalk in 1870. But Atlantic City managed to snare the honors of boardwalk originator.

The Promenade is often filled with folks strolling, jogging, walking dogs, and just hanging out. Bicycles are allowed from 4 A.M. to 10 A.M. It's also a great place to relax on one of the numerous benches and enjoy the cool ocean breezes. The Promenade has a center with a few food stands, a candy shop, some clothing stores, an arcade, and a gift shop. Nearby are numerous coin boxes selling newspapers. Public restrooms are located in the center but are open irregular hours except during the busy summer beach season, when they pretty much follow the beach hours.

Close to the Promenade stores is Convention Hall, which is the site of numerous special events and activities throughout the year. The Promenade also has two excellent restaurants: Henry's on the Beach, a family-style eatery, and Vanthia's, which offers fine dining.

If you have thrill-seeking kids and are looking for a boardwalk packed with amusements and rides, you won't find it in Cape May. But don't despair: Just a few miles north is Wildwood, which has a boardwalk with more amusements than boards.

In the summer, the Atlantic Ocean beach is packed with vacationers, eager to relax and spend some quality "me" time away from work. Yet the beach is long enough that the bathers are not packed like sardines broiling in suntan oil. At night, treasure hunters sometimes ply their trade, hoping that their metal detectors might reward them with a find. Nighttime activity on the beach

The Cape May Promenade winds along the beach, providing an inviting path for walkers, joggers, and bicyclists. PAT KING-ROBERTS

Cape May's surf and scenery attract beachgoers throughout the summer. SPIRIT CATCHER PHOTOGRAPHY

is discouraged, however, and you will get chased off if spotted.

In winter, the birds and solitary strollers take over. Each moves along the beach with head down against the chill winds whipping off the ocean, lost in his or her own thoughts. Occasionally the birds venture up to the wisps of eelgrass that have been planted near the Promenade in the hopes—mostly vain up to this point—of retaining sand against the next fearsome winter storm or hurricane.

Cape May's Atlantic Ocean beaches are eroding almost as fast as an ice cube in the summer sun. Only recent replenishment projects have helped build the beaches back up to a semblance of what they once were. A combination of factors are to blame, including global warming and the subsequent rise in sea level, development, and the movement of sand in the water near the coastline.

Visual evidence of this sand movement can easily be seen. Anyone who has ever been to the beach at Wildwood knows that if you want to get to the ocean after you place your towel down, you'd better start early in the day, and bring a snack. That's because the Wildwood beaches have been growing at an enormous rate, sometimes seeming to increase in size hourly. Why is this? Perhaps the simplest explanation has to do with the ill-conceived idea of building those stone piers, known as groins or jetties, into the ocean along the Cape May shoreline and at Cape May inlet. These man-made structures seriously disrupted the natural movement of sand up and down the coastline. Every time a storm chews off some more of the Cape May beach, the stone creations artificially disrupt the eventual natural return of the sand to Cape May. The result is that much of Cape May's sand has been adding to Wildwood's beaches. So when you're walking on the beach at Wildwood today, there's a good chance you're actually walking on Cape May sand.

Development has dramatically accelerated the erosion problem by flattening sand dunes and removing protective vegetation, and as one of the earliest shore resorts developed, Cape May has had more than its share of erosion problems. One estimate held that Cape May lost 169 feet of beach in about twenty years in the early 1800s. At some places it was even more severe, up to 300 feet. Erosion has taken a steady toll throughout the years on what was once a superior beach. In fact, even in the early twentieth century, the Cape May beach was so wide that its smooth, hard sand

A lifeguard stand is a relaxing perch after the midday beach crowds have left. SPIRIT CATCHER PHOTOGRAPHY

became one of the premier auto-racing sites on the East Coast. Only its relatively short length kept it from becoming a serious race site.

In the summer of 1905, four pioneers of the automobile–Louis Chevrolet, Henry Ford, Walter Christie, and A. L. Campbell–got together on the beach at Cape May for a race before a crowd estimated at 20,000. Ford took a quick lead, but a pesky ocean wave hit his car, knocking him awry. Campbell wound up winning, with Ford finishing dead last.

Finishing last was only the beginning of Ford's troubles. He needed the first-place prize money to pay his bill at Cape May's Stockton Hotel. Suddenly out of cash, he quickly had to sell a touring car to a man on board a train just pulling out of the Cape May train station. Ford concluded the transaction as he was running alongside the train. But when he got the check, he was told that the bank couldn't cash it because he lacked verification of his identity. Obviously Ford was having a

---

Visiting Cape May Beaches

Beach season: Memorial Day weekend to Labor Day weekend.
Hours: 10 A.M. to 5 P.M. daily.
Beach badges: Seasonal, $19; weekly, $11; three-day, $8; daily, $4.
Activities and Facilities: Swimming, boardwalk, accommodations, beach fires (permits required), fishing, surfing.
Payment: Credit cards not accepted. Send a check if desiring to pay in advance; otherwise, pay in person with cash or a check.
Bicycle paths: None.
Bicycle hours on the boardwalk/promenade: 4 A.M. to 10 A.M.
Surfing beaches: Colonial Beach and Jefferson Beach.
Surf-fishing beaches: All after 5 P.M.
Public boat ramps: None.
Fishing piers: None. Fishing off jetty at 2nd Ave.
Telephone: 609-884-5508.

bad day. Incidentally, the man who bought the car, Dan Focer, wound up becoming the first Ford automobile dealer in America.

Besides the Atlantic Ocean beach, Cape May also has beaches on the Delaware Bay side of town. Most notable of these are Higbee Beach and the beach at Cape May Point State Park (see page 32). Higbee Beach is primarily a preserved natural area and a great spot for birding. It is mainly a mixture of field, brush, and woods. It used to be known as a clothing-optional beach, but authorities have cracked down on that in recent years. At the state park you can hunt for Cape May "diamonds," watch a glorious sunset, see a haunted World War II bunker, and even view the sunken remnants of a true oddity: a battleship made out of concrete.

CAPE MAY COUNTY ZOO

Lions and tigers and bears . . . oh my!

With apologies to Dorothy from *The Wizard of Oz*, the Cape May County Park and Zoo has all those animals and a lot more.

Cape May is one of the few counties in New Jersey to have its very own zoo—and what a zoo! Far more than just a few sad-looking peacocks and monkeys sitting forlornly about, this is a world-class facility with hundreds of animals just off Exit 11 of the Garden State Parkway. Best of all, it's free, although donations are greatly appreciated and certainly deserved, as this is an excellent facility.

The Cape May County Zoo sprawls over more than 80 of the 128 acres in Cape May County Park. Half a million visitors per year visit this facility, which offers more than 200 species of mammals, birds, amphibians, and reptiles. The zoo adds new animals all the time and constantly refines and retools exhibits.

Another nice thing about the zoo is the amount of shade it provides, with large trees lining many of the pathways—refreshing on a hot summer day and affording protection from the sun for everybody from babies in strollers to the elderly. It is also an extraordinarily clean facility.

The zoo animals are in natural settings, with plenty of grass, shrubbery, and dirt. There are no animals in cages with concrete floors here. The zoo is also lined with asphalt pathways to make it easy to get around, so mothers with baby carriages and seniors with canes or walkers can navigate it with ease.

People go to the zoo to see the animals, and the Cape May Zoo doesn't disappoint. Besides lions, tigers, and bears, the zoo has camels, bison, alligators, leopards, cheetahs, ocelots, a giraffe named Jerome, more monkeys and monkey relatives than you can shake a banana at, tortoises, and an aviary exhibit with both exotic birds and local species. The zoo also has an impressive variety of unusual animals, including wallabies from Australia named Hanna and Kiwi, oryxes, kookaburras, and reindeer.

The Reptile House is an example of how well the county takes care of its zoo. The original structure was destroyed by a fire in the mid-1990s. It would have been easy at that point for the county to not rebuild it, citing the typical government

Visiting the Cape May County Zoo

4 Moore Rd., Garden State Parkway Exit 11, (mailing address: DN 801)
Cape May Court House, NJ 08210
Telephone: 609-465-5271 • Fax: 609-465-5421
Website: www.co.cape-may.nj.us

Hours: Daily except Christmas, 10 A.M. to 3:45 P.M. (4:45 P.M. in the summer). The African Savanna Bridge, World of Birds, and Amphibian and Reptile House close fifteen minutes earlier. Bad weather or related hazards such as fallen limbs may cause the zoo to close.

Admission: Free. Donations accepted.

Tours: Guided two-hour tours available. Schools and organizations outside Cape May County: $100 for one to twenty people, $5 for each additional person. Schools and organizations within Cape May County: $80 for one to twenty people, $3 for each additional person. No charge for one chaperone per ten students.

Shop: The zoo gift shop sells books, stuffed animals, and a variety of other souvenir items.

litany of lack of funds and "making the hard choices" to fund essential services at the expense of quality-of-life items. But no. Cape May County not only immediately rebuilt the Reptile House, but made it bigger and better than before. Now the house contains a variety of creepy-crawlies such as snakes and lizards, as well as an exhibit on endangered species of New Jersey so that kids and adults may take away a greater appreciation of the crush for space in this tightly packed world of ours.

One of the most interesting sections of the zoo is the African Savanna region. Here you walk on a giant elevated boardwalk built in a circular shape as you look at zebras, antelopes, giraffes, and numerous other animals associated with the African plains roaming over a large, grassy area very similar to their natural habitat. The feeling is definitely one of being on equal terms with the animals, avoiding that typical zoo feeling of watcher and watched. In fact, it's not uncommon to be on the same visual level as some of the animals as they meander by. It's probably

A giraffe is just one of the animals you can see in the African Savanna section of the Cape May County Zoo. CAPE MAY COUNTY PARK AND ZOO/CAPE MAY COUNTY COMMUNICATIONS DEPARTMENT

Monkeys are among the most popular attractions at the Cape May County Zoo. CAPE MAY COUNTY PARK AND ZOO/CAPE MAY COUNTY COMMUNICATIONS DEPARTMENT

the only time in your life you can look a giraffe straight in the eye!

The zoo is so large, and has so many animals, that you should plan on spending several hours here, perhaps even the entire day. It is open every day except Christmas. Hours vary seasonally. The zoo also features a café and a gift shop filled with stuffed animals and other souvenirs.

A visit to the Cape May Zoo is a great alternative to the beach. It's a place you can take kids in lieu of a boardwalk and makes an enjoyable day for the entire family.

CAPE MAY LIGHTHOUSE

If you spend any time at all in Cape May, you're bound to notice numerous brown street signs scattered about town with a picture of a lighthouse. Follow them through West Cape May to neighboring Lower Township, and you'll find yourself at one of Cape May's most popular and majestic attractions—the Cape May Lighthouse. It's just a few miles from the center of Cape May to the lighthouse, which is in Cape May Point State Park. There is ample free parking across the street in the park's parking lot.

The lighthouse is very tall—158 feet high—and very white. In keeping with nineteenth-century reasoning that every lighthouse had to be painted a different color so that it could be identified visually at sea, the Cape May Lighthouse is completely white except for some red at the top. It does not contain a keeper's shack nearby, as others of this style do, such as the Absecon Lighthouse in nearby Atlantic City.

What the Cape May Lighthouse does contain, however, is steps—218 of them, to be exact. That's a lot of climbing, with just a few places en route to the top to stop and rest. And if you're claustrophobic, remember that the people who went up before you have to come down the same way, so there's a lot of getting up close and personal with strangers on a rather narrow stairwell.

If your knees tremble at the thought of all those metal steps to climb and descend, there's a visitors orientation center called the Oil House at the bottom of the lighthouse where you can learn about its history. It also has a small gift shop filled with nautical knickknacks such as lighthouse statues, as well as toys and souvenirs.

But if you do climb, the view (which is pretty much the only reason for climbing to the top of a lighthouse, right?) from the top is simply spectacular. To one side are the roofs of nearby homes, looking tiny and insignificant from that high

The Cape May Lighthouse is one of the enduring symbols of the area. CRAIG TERRY

Visiting the Cape May Lighthouse

Lighthouse Ave., Cape May Point State Park
Cape May Point, NJ 08212
Telephone: 609-884-5404 or 800-275-4278
Website: www.capemaymac.org/Lighthouse

Hours: April through November, daily; hours vary throughout the year.
December through March, weekends only (call ahead for precise hours).
Admission: $5 adults, children twelve and under $1.
Credit cards: All major credit cards accepted.
Personal checks: Accepted for advance ticket orders only.
Shop: The Oil House contains a small gift shop with nautical memorabilia, toys,
   books, T-shirts, and other items.

up. Another side reveals the looming hulk of the Concrete Bunker, built during World War II, when it was feared that Nazi submarines were about to come popping out of the water just offshore. If you look hard enough, and in the right place, you can even see the slowly sinking remnants of the infamous concrete ship.

Trumping everything, however, are the shimmering blue-green waters of the Atlantic Ocean, which stretch away from the lighthouse as far as the eye can see.

The lighthouse is the third such structure built around the site. The first two locations are now underwater, an illustration of the power of erosion and the rising sea levels. There is anecdotal evidence that there may have been a lighthouse there as early as the 1700s, but there is no historical data to support that claim.

Another popular belief is that George Meade, savior of the Union during the Civil War at Gettysburg, was involved in the building of the Cape May Lighthouse. Meade was involved in two Jersey Shore lighthouses, but they were Barnegat Light on Long Beach Island and Absecon, not Cape May.

The lighthouse is another attraction operated and administered by MAC. The last lightkeeper retired in the 1930s. Thereafter, the Coast Guard ran the light until MAC took over in 1986, by which point the structure was in desperate need of maintenance. MAC has spent more than $2 million since 1988 restoring the lighthouse. Included in that effort has been lead paint removal, restoration of the lantern, and painting. The result is a beautifully restored lighthouse that brings back romantic memories of the days of old, when lighthouses and their dedicated

The beacon light at the top of the Cape May Lighthouse is still operational. KYLE WEAVER

keepers were all that stood between a ship and its foundering on sudden sandbars and other unseen obstacles submerged in the water.

According to MAC's lighthouse manager Rich Chimiengo, the lighthouse gets about 100,000 climbers per year, and about twice that, or 200,000 people, visit the historic structure. Chimiengo reports that the biggest maintenance headaches are painting and sweeping the sand out of the structure. Visitors often are dismayed to find out that the lighthouse doesn't have an elevator. And although Cape May seems to be a rather active town for supernatural activity, ghosts seem to have skipped the lighthouse. Perhaps they're also annoyed by the lack of an elevator.

CAPE MAY POINT STATE PARK

Tiny but mighty describes this state park at the very tip of New Jersey, just across from the Cape May Lighthouse. Although it is one of the smallest parks in the state park system, Cape May Point offers a wealth of things to do.

For hiking and nature enthusiasts, the park has several trails, from short and easy (half a mile) to longer and tougher (two miles). At any time on the trails, depending on the time of day, season, and weather conditions, you may encounter otters, muskrats, ducks, frogs, turtles, wading birds, monarch butterflies, and even an occasional osprey, as well as numerous types of plant life. There are observation platforms for viewing, and if you remain on the platforms and are very still, you may well be rewarded with a wildlife sighting. Some of the trails go by ponds, which come alive in the summer with the sound of croaking bullfrogs. Sometimes you can see turtles sunning themselves.

The shortest trail, known as the Red Trail, is wheelchair-accessible, which is rare for nature trails. Elevated boardwalks go across boggy areas to keep the wheels from getting mired down. The trails go through several different types of terrain as you wander over them, from boggy to sandy to hard earth. One trail even goes by the nearby beach, and if there is not too much human activity taking place, you may be rewarded with shorebird sightings.

Going in wetter weather means more mud and softer ground, even in areas not served by boardwalks. Going in drier weather doesn't guarantee that you won't run into mud, but you have a better chance of keeping your Hush Puppies from getting mud-caked. No matter when you go, use bug repellent, because there are many biting insects, not to mention ticks.

In the autumn, from roughly mid-September to late October, thousands of monarch butterflies stop at the park on their way south. It is truly a breathtaking sight to see all those butterflies in one small area, wings twitching and ready for flight. When a pack of them rises into the air, it is like a dark orange cloud blocking out the sun.

From just after the heat of the summer until winter's first chill, approximately mid-September until mid-November, Cape May Point State Park is the best place on the eastern seaboard to see migrating hawks. Thousands of birders head to the park at this time. But birders flock to the park at other times of the year as well, because of its location on the migratory routes of many different species. Whenever you go, you may be able to spot a variety of birds.

The Cape May Rips, an area of strong currents offshore near the park, is also well known for excellent birding. Almost any day you can see birds feeding in the Rips, which can produce unexpected surprises. Midwinter may bring razorbills or northern fulmars, and summer has seen the appearance of sooty, cory's, and greater shearwaters. One of the rarest birds ever, a whiskered tern, was first found after it came in from the Rips to rest on the beach in 1993. To bird the Rips, set up a spotting scope on the beach at the park and look south.

The park's beach area on the Atlantic Ocean is nice and wide, and though no swimming is allowed, it is perfect for sunbathing or surf fishing, as long as you don't mind sharing your sand with the gulls that frequently land and scurry around, looking for food.

Another point of interest in the park stands very creakily in the surf on the beach. It is the Cape May Bunker, built in 1942 at the height of wartime hysteria over a submarine invasion. The bunker hasn't been in use for many years, and it looks it: Birds perch on the stained and dirty hulking concrete structure, while the wood pilings it sits on are green with algae and age and look as if they're about to collapse into the foaming surf just beyond. There are big signs posted warning Keep Off, but who'd want to go on? If Dracula were in the Army, this is where he'd be stationed.

There are rumors that the bunker is haunted. If it isn't, it certainly looks as though it should be. Usually around sundown, people supposedly see figures mov-

The imposing World War II–era Cape May bunker served as a surveillance post. PAT KING-ROBERTS

Visiting Cape May Point State Park

Lighthouse Ave., Cape May Point State Park
(mailing address: P.O. Box 107), Cape May Point, NJ 08212
Telephone: 609-884-2159

Hours: Dawn to dusk.
Admission: Free.
Programs: Hawk-banding demonstrations every Saturday and Sunday at 10 A.M.,
  mid-September to mid-October. Guided nature walks and bird walks from late
  spring into autumn. Children's nature clubs and programs are held during the
  summer; call for a schedule of events.

---

ing about on top of the bunker out of the corner of their eye. Some folks even faintly hear shouted military commands wafting in the ocean breezes. But if you turn and stare at the bunker, there is nobody to be seen.

The park also contains an interpretive center, a small museum, and a touch tank for kids. It has no concessions, but there are two picnic pavilions, one with tables overlooking the ocean and another by the trails and hawk-watch platform. Parking is free in a large lot.

SUNSET BEACH

Sunset Beach is a small beach with several souvenir and food huts, located at the foot of Sunset Boulevard on Delaware Bay. A trip here provides the visitor with surprising rewards. Swimming is not allowed at Sunset Beach, but you'll find Cape May "diamonds," a concrete ship, and an extraordinarily moving sunset flag ceremony.

If you spend any time at all in Cape May, you'll certainly hear the term "Cape May diamonds." These are not real diamonds, however, but pieces of pure quartz crystal that can be polished to a diamondlike sheen. They come from eroded pockets and veins of pure quartz located in the upper reaches of the Delaware River several hundred miles away. Once freed from their rock prison, they travel down to the ocean, usually taking thousands of years to make the trip. When they reach the mouth of the Delaware Bay, the strong intersecting currents from the two colliding bodies of water—ocean and bay—whip them around, smooth and polish them, and eventually throw them onto the shore at Sunset Beach.

Found in different shapes and sizes ranging from pebbles to eggs, Cape May diamonds have been around as long as there have been people in the region. The Kechemeche Indians believed that they possessed magical powers. King Nummy of the Lenni-Lenape gave one to an early settler, who sent it back to Holland. There it was cut and polished into a beautiful gem that resembled a diamond, and Cape May diamonds were born.

People constantly scour Sunset Beach for these unusual stones, and when you visit, you'll often find more people with their eyes downcast than at a funeral. The smaller stones tend to wash up in the summer, and the heavier winter surf brings the bigger ones ashore.

Because of things like atmospheric conditions, the sun angle at the horizon, and lots of other scientific gobbledygook, the sunsets here are spectacular—vivid and awe-inspiring. The fading sun often resembles a fiery red ball as it sinks toward the horizon like a red-hot coal about to be extinguished in a bucket of water.

Every summer evening at sunset, from May through September, an evening flag ceremony is held that's not to be missed. A different flag is flown every night, and each is from the casket of an American soldier who lost his or her life in defense of this country. As the fiery sun slowly sinks into Delaware Bay, the American flag is lowered by a uniformed honor guard while Kate Smith singing "God Bless America" warbles through the speakers atop telephone poles. People sing, salute the flag, hold each other, and cry. It is incredibly emotional, particularly because the family of the soldier being honored is usually present. It is a simple yet moving ceremony, helped in no small part by the majesty of the sun fading into the horizon. You can't leave Cape May without experiencing this ceremony at least once. *Note:* Parking at Sunset Beach is limited, and the ceremony is well attended. Plan to come early, or you're going to wind up parking well up on Sunset Boulevard.

Another thing to do at Sunset Beach is gaze out at the remnants of a unique American original and a rapidly disappearing oddity: a freighter ship made out of concrete. Yes, concrete.

Called the *Atlantus*, it was part of an experimental fleet of World War I ships made out of concrete because of a steel shortage. Thirty-eight such vessels were planned, but only twelve were ever built and put into service. The *Atlantus* was the second prototype. She weighed 3,000 tons, was 250 feet long, and had a five-inch-thick hull.

Launched on November 21, 1918, the *Atlantus* served for a year as a coal steamer. With the end of the war, steel was again plentiful, and the heavy, awkward concrete ships were quickly decommissioned. (Try pushing a cement block around your bathtub for a similar experience.) By 1926, the *Atlantus* was wasting away in Virginia, when it was bought by a Baltimore company and towed to Cape May as part of a plan to begin ferry serv-

The Sunset Beach flag ceremony is a beautiful tribute to America's fallen fighting men and women. PAT KING-ROBERTS

At some point in the not-too-distant future, the concrete ship *Atlantus* will completely disappear from view. KYLE WEAVER

ice between Cape May and Lewes, Delaware. The ship was to be used as part of the ferry dock.

But fate had other plans. While awaiting its final resting place, the *Atlantus* was hit by a fierce storm in June 1926. The ship broke free from its moorings, wandered a bit out into the open water, and went aground, sinking like a concrete block in the very spot it's in today. Since then, neither man nor miracle has been able to move it. Every year, a bit more of it disappears under water as it settles a little farther into the sand at the bottom of the bay. Right now just a fraction of the massive concrete ship that was once visible can be seen. Try looking at some of the post-

---

Visiting Sunset Beach

Sunset Beach Gift Shops, 502 Sunset Blvd.
(mailing address: P.O. Box 485), Cape May Point, NJ 08212
Telephone: 609-884-7079 • Fax: 609-884-6468
E-mail: gifts@sunsetbeachnj.com • Website: www.sunsetbeachnj.com

Hours: 9 A.M. to sunset in summer. Winter hours vary; call ahead.
Credit cards: Visa, MasterCard, and American Express accepted.
Personal checks: not accepted.

cards from years past that are available for sale at various stores throughout Cape May to get an idea of how much of the ship used to be visible. In forty years or less, the whole thing may be underwater.

There are three gift shops at Sunset Beach that sell everything from plastic rings to nautical collectibles. If your search for Cape May diamonds gets you hungry, you can head over to the Sunset Beach Grill for a hot dog or a burger.

EMLEN PHYSICK ESTATE

In 1879, a house was built in Cape May that caused a bit of a stir. It was built in the avant-garde stick style, which was unusual for that era. Even more unusual was the man who inhabited the home, Dr. Emlen Physick, who–despite being called "doctor" and having a medical degree–didn't have to practice as a physician thanks to an inheritance. So he did what most of us would do if we inherited a pile of money: He retired and built an opulent house, where he lived a life of luxury. Little did he dream that more than a century later, his grand home would be the focal point of a bustling resort community.

The opulent Emlen Physick estate, one of the most spectacular homes of its time, is now open to the public. MID-ATLANTIC CENTER FOR THE ARTS

Visiting the Emlen Physick Estate

1048 Washington St., Cape May, NJ 08204
Phone: 609-884-5404 or 800-275-4278 • Fax: 609-884-2006
E-mail: mac4arts@capemaymac.org. • Website: www.capemaymac.org

Hours: Mid-June through mid-September, daily, 9:30 A.M. to 5 P.M.; mid-September through December, daily, 11 A.M. to 4 P.M.; January through mid-March, weekends, 10 A.M. to 3 P.M.; mid-March through April, Sunday through Friday, 11 A.M. to 3 P.M., Saturday, 10 A.M. to 5 P.M.; May through mid-June, daily, 10:30 A.M. to 4:30 P.M.

Tours: House tours daily, $10 for adults, $5 for children; Carriage House Gallery, $4. Garden tours also available. For group tours, contact MAC, P.O. Box 340, Cape May, NJ 08204, telephone 609-884-5404 or 800-275-4278, ext. 139, fax 609-884-2006.

Programs: Hours and schedule vary, call for details. Special events include six weeks of holiday festivities, annual Victorian fair, and Kids' Day.

The Physick Estate has the only historic house museum tour in Cape May that operates daily. Although this may be hard to believe in a town with so many historic homes, it's true. Other homes may let visitors tour as part of a larger or previously defined group or tour package, but only the Physick Estate runs regularly scheduled tours all day, every day for guests.

The Physick House, with its distinctive orange-red shingles, sits on a slight incline back from Washington Street and is the centerpiece of a complex that is home to the

Mid-Atlantic Center for the Arts (MAC). The other small outbuildings in the compound are MAC offices. The Carriage House, which is the first building you encounter when you turn into the Physick House driveway from Washington Street, houses a small tea-oriented gift shop and the Carriage House Tearoom, an exceptional restaurant. It also contains a gallery with changing exhibits about past life in Cape May. The subject can be anything from World War II to life in the 1960s, before it became a Victorian resort. There is a small fee for viewing the display. The amount of time it takes to view the display is however long it takes you to read the items.

People in Victorian garb are a common sight during Victorian Week. MID-ATLANTIC CENTER FOR THE ARTS

Even kids get into the Victorian spirit in Cape May. MID-ATLANTIC CENTER FOR THE ARTS

When the door opens to begin the hourlong tour of the Physick Estate, you never quite know what's going to happen. Sometimes a MAC guide takes you through rooms in the house and explains their function in the life of the Physick family. But sometimes either Physick's mother or maiden aunt, both of whom lived there with him, appears and conducts the tours in the first person, as if the doctor has just stepped out for a moment and will be coming back shortly. The reenactor, in full period clothing, is delightfully off-center and never breaks character, making for a fun and unusual tour for everyone, particularly when she makes throwaway comments about the times or the family.

The tour winds all over the three-story, eighteen-room house, from the game room with its billiard table on the third floor to the dining room and kitchen on the first floor, as the guide points out objects of interest. The inside of the home is decorated in typical Victorian fashion, with plenty of flowered wallpaper, lace doilies, pictures, and decorative objects on tables and chairs. According to the curator, the estate's Elizabeth Reighn, about 25 percent of the furniture in the home is authentic, and the rest is correct to the period. Inside the house, surrounded by all these Victorian furnishings and with the outside noises shut out, it could well be 1890.

The house has been attributed to noted architect Frank Furness, although no historical documentation exists to verify this. If so, it is one of the few unaltered Furness structures in existence, a fact that excites the architect's fans. What is not widely known is that Furness supposedly designed much of the inside too, such as the molding and fireplaces.

After Physick died in 1916, the house went through a variety of owners and became so dilapidated it looked like the stereotypical haunted house by 1970. Slated to be torn down by developers to make room for tract housing, the house became a rallying point for citizens who had a vision that Cape May could become the Victorian Jewel of the Jersey Shore. MAC was formed, the house was saved, and Cape May has not looked back.

Initially the estate was so vast that it reached nearly to the ocean several blocks east. Time and development have whittled that area down to its present size, but the house is still going strong, having survived surprisingly well after all these years of tours and thousands of pairs of visiting feet. Reighn says the house is really well built, and her biggest maintenance headache is painting.

Somewhere Doctor Physick is smiling, and perhaps Frank Furness as well.

CAPE MAY CARRIAGE COMPANY

Horse-drawn carriages seem to epitomize the Victorian era. In every Sherlock Holmes story, in every illustration about Queen Victoria, in everything that's anything Victorian, a horse-drawn carriage typically is present. So what could be more perfect when visiting Victorian Cape May than traveling around the city in a horse-drawn carriage?

Enter the Cape May Carriage Company, which provides precisely that. If you go to the Washington Street Mall when you're in Cape May—and you almost certainly will—you'll find the horses lined up on Ocean Street next to Washington Commons. This is the small shopping cluster across the mall side from the MAC Information Booth and the Star of the Sea church. You can usually find three or four horse-drawn carriages there, waiting patiently for their next riders. Their drivers are also close by, making sure no overexuberant visitor tries to feed the horses an ice cream cone or candy apple. *Note:* This is the *only* location at which you can purchase carriage ride tickets.

The Cape May Carriage Company offers, weather permitting, half-hour narrated tours on weekends during the spring and fall and daily tours during the sum-

The clip-clop of horse hooves is a familiar sound in the Cape May Historic District. MID-ATLANTIC CENTER FOR THE ARTS

Taking a Cape May Carriage Ride

641 Sunset Blvd., Cape May, NJ 08204
Telephone: 609-884-4466 • E-mail: CapeMayCarriage@msn.com
Website: www.capemaycarriage.com

Hours: Carriage rides are available, weather permitting, from April through May and October through November, Friday 6 to 10 P.M., Saturday 11 A.M. to 3 P.M. and 6 to 10 P.M., Sunday 11 A.M. to 3 P.M. and 6 to 10 P.M.; and June 1 through October 1, daily, 10 A.M. to 3 P.M. and 6 to 10:30 P.M. Holiday season hours are from November 24 through December 23, Friday 5 to 10 P.M., Saturday, 11 A.M. to 10 P.M., and Sunday, 11 A.M. to 9 P.M. December 26 through 31, hours are daily, 11 A.M. to 10 P.M.

Rates: Private carriages, $40 for two passengers, additional adult $10, additional child two to eleven $5. Group tours: $10 per adult, $5 per child age two to eleven.

Credit cards: Not accepted.

Personal checks: Not accepted.

mer and Christmas season. Various themed tours are available, including one that goes through the adjacent city of West Cape May. The most popular tour is probably the one that meanders through the Historic District. The driver explains the history behind many of the homes on the tour and also answers any questions you may have. Some people bring snacks, such as wine and cheese, to further enhance the experience. The carriages can comfortably fit up to six people.

There is no better way to see this jewel of a city than from the seat of a horse-drawn carriage. The horses amble along, following no schedule but their own, as the driver relates the sights, sounds, and stories of Cape May. The drivers are friendly, personable, and knowledgeable. Seeing the homes at the horses' pace allows you to fully appreciate the beauty and detail of their craftsmanship.

But Cape May is just that kind of city—meant to be enjoyed at a slower pace than the frantic rush of modern life. It is a place where the gentle clip-clop of horses' hooves and the creak of rocking chairs on the front porch seem not only appropriate, but necessary. As you travel around in the horse and carriage, cars push by, some drivers angrily looking at the horse as a cumbersome roadblock as kids peer fascinated out of the back window. But it doesn't matter. Shut your eyes and it's 1885 once again.

Cape May Carriage Company owner Becky Alexander, a former driver who bought the business a few years ago, says they have nineteen working horses, of which they run two during the day and nine at night during peak times. The horses work only five days a week. According to Alexander, horses go through a two- to five-month training period before being permitted to go out onto the Cape May streets. The farm where the horses live during their off-time—and enjoy bubble baths!—houses a fleet of draft horses such as Belgian, Percheron, and crossbreeds. And just like people, the horses all have their own personalities.

A tour in a horse-drawn carriage is an excellent way to take in the slow pace and historic ambience.
MID-ATLANTIC CENTER FOR THE ARTS

"Horses are smart animals, and they definitely have minds of their own," says Diana, one of the drivers. Although the horses are used to the cars that move around them, some take more notice of traffic than others. According to Diana, among the questions visitors ask most frequently are "Is it a real horse?" "How do you turn them?" and "Who changes the horse's diaper?"

"This is a good job," Diana adds cheerfully, "especially if you like horses."

HISTORIC COLD SPRING VILLAGE

Trying to explain to kids what life was like more than a century ago is like trying to cut steak with a plastic knife. It is difficult to describe a world with few entertainment options—except using your imagination and reading—to someone growing up in today's fast-paced electronic, TV, and video-game culture.

But a picture is worth a thousand words, and Historic Cold Spring Village is just that picture. With twenty-five restored buildings on twenty-two acres in a beautiful wooded area just outside Cape May, it depicts what life was like in an early to mid-nineteenth-century South Jersey village, in the period between the American Revolution and the Civil War. Each building is dedicated to a specific craft, such as weaving, printing, quilting, broom making, or blacksmithing, with costumed interpreters who explain the tasks they are performing.

More than thirty years ago, Cape May County began bringing these old buildings from all over the county to the site to preserve them rather than to let developers destroy them. Thanks to the county's foresight, today the site is an open-air history museum that's fun and educational for one and all.

The village is not very spread out, so it's easy to get from one building to another. No cars are allowed in the village, so you don't have to worry about your kids crossing the road. The site is extraordinarily shady, refreshing during those hot months when the summer sun is beating down. You tour the village at your own pace, so you can spend a few hours there or a whole day. The buildings are named for easy reference. The Philip Hand House, for example, is where the weaver operates.

The interpreters, dressed in period clothing, are lively and informative as they share information about their tasks. With infinite patience, they answer, instruct, and demonstrate how our ancestors lived during this time period. No question seems beyond their scope of knowledge or too silly to be answered, such as "Are the sheep hurt when you cut off their wool?" "No, just chilly."

Sometimes interpreters invite visitors to help them with their tasks, much to the delight of the children present. Watching a twenty-first-century technophile trying to do a relatively simple manual task, such as fastening together the strands of a broom or moving printing type around, is interesting–and often amusing.

It can be fascinating to watch the kids' faces at the Old School House. The teacher, usually a female, is dressed in period clothing, such as a wool dress and bonnet–a far cry from today's slacks or skirts. When kids used to today's modern, airy buildings enter the small, stuffy room with tiny wooden desks, you can read their minds in their faces: "I'm glad I wasn't born back then!" And when the teacher relates the concept of corporal punishment instead of detention, the relief on the kids' faces that they are in the here and now is palpable.

Visiting Historic Cold Spring Village

720 Rt. 9, Cape May, NJ 08204
Telephone: 609-898-2300• Website: www.hcsv.org

Hours: 10 A.M. to 4:30 P.M., weekends from Memorial Day weekend through June 20; Tuesday through Sunday until Labor Day weekend; and then weekends until mid-September.

Admission: Adults $8; senior citizens $7, children three to twelve $5, under three free.

Credit cards: Visa or MasterCard.

Personal checks: Accepted.

Educational programs: Topics include the history of the U.S. flag, a typical school day for children in 1800, and the day of a typical mother in 1800. For information, contact Jim Stephens, education coordinator, telephone 609-898-2300, ext. 17, e-mail jstephens@hcsv.org.

Shop: Besides buying ice cream at the Old Fashioned Ice Cream Parlor and baked goods at the bakery, you can also buy candles, penny candy, yarn, and other items at the General Store. The Museum Shop sells more traditional souvenirs such as mugs.

A visitors center sets the stage when you arrive at the village and gives plenty of historical information, both with displayed objects and through a video presentation. There are also several food options on-site, ranging from hamburgers and hot dogs, ice cream, and a bakery to a sit-down restaurant.

Historic Cold Spring Village is just five minutes outside of Cape May on Route 9. You'll find plenty of free parking at both village entrances.

NATURE CENTER OF CAPE MAY

With all the Victorian hoopla that surrounds Cape May, it can be easy to forget that it is still a seacoast town, with the environmental responsibility that comes with living and playing in a town so close to the life-giving ocean. Children are the future caregivers of the planet, and the Nature Center of Cape May directs its dual message of ecological awareness and fun primarily at them. Adults, however, will also find things here to interest them.

The Nature Center consists of a group of nondescript buildings on Delaware Avenue that look like anything but what they are—a place that provides a cluster of exciting experiences for kids. The Nature Center was founded in 1992 and adopted by the New Jersey Audubon Society in 1995. Besides providing environmental education for children and adults, the museum is also trying to create a feeling of personal responsibility for the open space around Cape May Harbor, which lies just across the street.

The Nature Center at Cape May teaches visitors about the environment in an entertaining, kid-friendly manner. PAT KING-ROBERTS

Visiting the Nature Center of Cape May

1600 Delaware Ave., Cape May, NJ 08204
Telephone: 609-898-8848• E-mail: nccm@njaudubon.org
Website: www.njaudubon.org/centers/NCCM

Hours: January through April, Tuesday through Saturday, 10 A.M. to 3 P.M.; May through September, daily, 10 A.M. to 4 P.M.; October through December, Tuesday through Saturday, 10 A.M. to 3 P.M. Open other times for special events and programs.
Admission: Free.
Credit cards: All major credit cards accepted.
Personal checks: Accepted.
Programs: Numerous programs for kids and adults. Call for details.
Shop: An attached gift shop sells books, stuffed animals, and other nature-oriented items.

Parking and admission are both free. There are no food facilities, but picnic tables are scattered about, so feel free to bring a lunch.

Inside, you'll find an extensive nature store that sells everything from books to plastic animal figures to clothes. In several large classroom buildings, kids can color, make pictures, read, and participate in other hands-on activities with a natural theme. Within these rooms are ever-changing seasonal exhibits of local sea-dwelling creatures, some of which come from the bay and natural area just across the street. At any one time you may see eels, baby jellyfish, turtles, minnows, and horseshoe, hermit, and blue crabs, among other animals.

Another interesting feature is the theme gardens located both in front and in back of the Nature Center. There is something quite magical about watching birds of all sizes and colors flocking to feeders and trees in the songbird garden in the dead of winter, when all life seems suspended. The butterfly garden is a riot of color and motion in the summer. Other theme gardens include seaside, shade, wetland, herb, drought-tolerant, and backyard habitat gardens. Some of the gardens can be seen from windows inside the hands-on activity rooms.

Activities for families with young ones sponsored by the Nature Center include the popular Harbor Safari. Here children, with the help of Nature Center staff, get to drag a seine net through the waters of Cape May Harbor and see the incredible variety of creatures that exist so close to shore. The staff then sets up touch tanks on the beach, so that kids and families can get a close-up look at what they've netted. Both kids and adults are usually surprised at the diversity of life, such as fish and crabs, that they have captured, along with the occasional old sneaker. In addition, they get information about the natural history of the harbor and some of the area. As part of the program, the staff also does demonstrations in the center's lab. For example, the kids may learn about live horseshoe crabs and their importance.

The Nature Center offers a large variety of fee-based daytime programs during the summer. It is advisable to sign up early, as they fill up rapidly, although the center usually keeps some spots open for last-minute arrivals. Nighttime programs are also offered, such as a ghost crab walk, in which participants walk along the beach and try to spot these elusive creatures as they scurry along.

The Nature Center of Cape May is the perfect example of something fun to do in Cape May for families with kids.

DESIGNER SHOW HOUSE

The Designer Show House enjoyed its inaugural season in 2005 as a Cape May attraction. The popular response was so great, the idea has returned in succeeding years, although in different houses and locations.

The Designer Show House is an architecturally significant home somewhere in Cape May that has been spectacularly renovated from top to bottom by a crew of professional designers. It can be toured until the owner comes to town after the season is over to set up permanent residence in it. In 2005, the home selected was a 1915 Craftsman-style Gustav Stickley structure on Washington Street across from the Washington Inn.

Stickley was an American furniture designer and architect who operated a chair factory in Binghamton, New York, in the 1880s. Around the turn of the century, he began producing sturdy, functional, and inexpensive oak pieces that broke from the Victorian tradition by emphasizing simplicity and functionality over complexity and ornamentation.

The former Franklin Street Church was featured as MAC's Designer Show House in 2006. MID-ATLANTIC CENTER FOR THE ARTS

Visiting the Designer Show House

Mid-Atlantic Center for the Arts (MAC), 1048 Washington St., Cape May, NJ 08204
Telephone: 609-884-5404 or 800-275-4278 • Fax: 609-884-2006
E-mail: mac4arts@capemaymac.org • Website: www.capemaymac.org

Cost: Contact MAC for the cost of tickets and other information.
Credit cards: All major credit cards accepted.
Personal checks: Accepted only for advance ticket orders.

His vision also carried over into home design. In 1901, he began publishing a magazine called *The Craftsman,* which brought his ideas to a whole new audience. He used the magazine to offer plans for houses that subscribers could obtain free. Stickley's goal was to offer the typical American family a home based on beauty, simplicity, utility, and harmony with its surroundings. He strove to replace expensive items with ones that were less expensive yet reflected good taste and to display beauty without excessive ornamentation.

The 2005 designer home was built in 1915 as a wedding gift for John Hewitt, a local merchant and banker, and his bride Mabel. Like all Craftsman homes, it relied on form, function, and structural elements for decorative details. Many of Stickley's philosophies were incorporated into the house, as reflected in the library's exposed beams and the exterior brickwork.

In 2006, a former church was transformed into a magnificent residence. In 2007, the home selected was the Memucan Hughes House, an 1847 pilot's house with eleven bedrooms, six bathrooms, formal parlors, covered porches, a huge dining room, a kitchen, a library, and a study. It was located on Hughes Street, in the midst of the Historic District in Cape May. Natural textured materials such as wood and brick provide interesting visual images when light hits them.

In November 2004, the house was purchased by its current owner, who agreed to let it be renovated and toured until after the season. MAC gathered together a team of interior decorators and designers from all over, including Philadelphia and Cape May, and let them loose. The result is one of the most beautiful homes you'll ever see short of Buckingham Palace.

Each room has been remodeled according to a specific theme. The living room, for example, is a tribute to William Morris, considered the father of the Arts and Crafts Movement. From the embossed leather painting style, which incorporates designs Morris developed in his own wallpaper, to the handmade lighting fixtures, the room is pure Morris. He also is represented in the theme for the guest suite known as the Strawberry Thief, the name of a famous Morris textile design. With its Jacuzzi tub, walk-in shower, and plasma screen television, the room will make guests wish they were permanent residents.

A MAC guide leads visitors through the home, pointing out various details. Each guest also receives a program book, which contains information about each room as well as the designers that created them . . . just in case he or she is thinking of trying the same thing at his or her house.

In 2005 and 2006, MAC offered an online buy one, get one free promotion for Designer Show House tickets. Also, a special Designer Show Dinner and House Tour was offered from Monday through Thursday both years. For $40 per person, guests got a three-course dinner and a glass of wine at the Washington Inn, followed by a guided tour of the Designer Show House. Check to see if these offers are still available.

FISHERMEN'S MEMORIAL

This isn't a place where you're going to spend a lot of time. It consists of just a statue, a memorial wall, and some benches, surrounded by trees and cattails. But if you're in the mood for a little quiet reflection, this tiny oasis is a good place to go.

The best way to get here is to head for Pittsburgh Avenue, which is one of the main routes in and out of town. Once on the road, look for brown signs for the Fishermen's Memorial. Don't expect anything on a massive scale. The parking lot has room for half a dozen cars, and there are no souvenir or food stands around, nor are there restrooms. This should underscore the notion that this isn't a typical tourist activity. It's just a small but heartfelt tribute to all those brave souls from Cape May who set out to wring a living from the unpredictable and sometimes deadly Atlantic Ocean and never came back.

The Fishermen's Memorial is reminiscent of the Vietnam Veterans Memorial in Washington, D.C. On a long stone wall at the memorial are listed the names of those lost at sea from Cape May, along with the year they disappeared. At the bottom of the shoulder-high structure, friends and family members have left little mementos for their lost loved ones, such as flowers and stuffed animals. In the middle of the memorial is a statue of a woman and her two small children, staring hopefully toward the water for the return of their loved one, who unfortunately will never come home again.

You can sit on one of the small stone benches to drink in the scene, or walk

The Fishermen's Memorial is a simple yet effective tribute to those who lost their lives at sea.
PAT KING-ROBERTS

Visiting the Fishermen's Memorial

Baltimore Ave. and Missouri Ave.
Cape May, NJ 08204

Hours: Dawn through dusk.

---

on the little beach to get right up close to the water. If you've ever admired the bravery of those who have dared to challenge the powerful ocean, especially in the early days, this is the place to go.

CAPE MAY FIRE DEPARTMENT MUSEUM

It won't take you a whole day to tour it, or even half a day. An hour should be sufficient here. But the Fireman's Hall History Museum at the intersection of Franklin and Washington Streets, one block from the pedestrian mall and catty-corner from the post office, is worth a look.

The building is not very big. It was built in 1984 to resemble a typical Victorian-era firehouse. There are no tour guides and usually few tourists in this donation-

This old-fashioned fire truck takes up most of the first floor of the Fire Department Museum. PAT KING-ROBERTS

Visiting the Cape May Fire Department Museum

643 Washington St., Cape May, NJ 08204

Admission: Free.
Hours: Irregular, particularly in the off-season.

supported museum. But if you're interested in fire equipment of the past, it's definitely worth a visit.

The museum contains firefighting equipment and fire department photos from past eras in Cape May's history. The items are displayed in glass cases on the walls and floor. The downstairs is set up to look like a fire station whose crew has left for just a moment and will be right back. A coat hangs on the back of a desk chair. On the desk are a telephone and various papers. It wouldn't be surprising to see a steaming cup of coffee cooling there as well.

Upstairs, a winding staircase takes you to a small balcony area that leads to the building's most interesting feature—a large tower straight out of a gothic novel. Unfortunately, the tower is not visitor-accessible. Back when the building was a working firehouse, the tower was used to hang up the fire hoses, stretch them out, and dry them.

The highlight of the museum, taking up 90 percent of the space on the bottom floor, is a restored 1928 American LaFrance fire truck, which was in service until 1964. You can't sit in it, ring the bells or blast the siren, or any of that fun stuff, but the gleaming red machine is a great piece of history that you can examine up close.

Hanging from the ceiling is a huge mural depicting a group of firemen readying a flag for hoisting in the midst of rubble. It is an acknowledgment of the fact that firefighters represent the best of America, people unselfishly ready to help others, such as on 9/11.

OTHER ATTRACTIONS

Historical Sites and Museums

Colonial House
653½ Washington St.
(behind Alexander's Restaurant)
Cape May, NJ 08204
Telephone: 609-884-9100
Website: www.capemayhistory.org
Hours: 10 A.M. to 2 P.M. daily from June 15
    to September 15.
Admission: By donation.
The Colonial House is home of the Greater Cape May Historical Society and the only Colonial-era house open to the public for tours.

Cold Spring Presbyterian Church
Rt. 9, north of Townbank Road
Cold Spring, NJ 08204
Telephone: 609-884-4065
This is one of the oldest churches in America and the burial site of more descendants of the *Mayflower* than are in Massachusetts.

Cape May County Historical Museum
504 Rt. 9 North
Cape May Court House, NJ 08210
Telephone: 609-465-3535
Website: www.cmcmuseum.org
The Cape May County Historical Museum, run by the Cape May County Historical and Genealogical Society, is housed in the Cresse-Holmes House, one of the oldest structures in Cape May County.

Aviation Museum
300 Forrestal Rd.
Cape May County Airport
Rio Grande, NJ 08242
Telephone: 609-886-8787
Website: www.usnasw.org
Hours: May through September, daily, 9 A.M. to 5 P.M.; October through April, daily, 9 A.M. to 4 P.M.
Admission: Adults $6; children 3 to 12 years old $3.
The Aviation Museum, also called Naval Air Station Wildwood, contains more than a dozen vintage aircraft from the World War II and Vietnam War eras.

Ferry

Cape May–Lewes Ferry
Sandman Blvd. and Lincoln Dr.
North Cape May, NJ 08204
Telephone: 800-643-3779 (reservations)
Website: www.capemaylewesferry.com
The ferry carries both people and autos between Cape May and Lewes, Delaware. The trip takes an hour and ten minutes each way.

Cape May Bird Observatory

Northwood Center
701 East Lake Dr.
P.O. Box 3 (mailing address)
Cape May Point, NJ 08212
Telephone: 609-884-2736
E-mail: cmbo1@njaudubon.org
Hours: 9 A.M. to 4:30 P.M. daily.

Center for Research and Education
600 Rt. 47 North
Cape May Court House, NJ 08210
Telephone: 609-861-0700
E-mail: cmbo2@njaudubon.org
Hours: 9 A.M. to 4:30 P.M. daily.

These two New Jersey Audubon Society facilities are dedicated to the spectacular natural world that is Cape May. The observatory also provides a birding hotline at 609-898-BIRD.

Wildlife Observation

Higbee Beach Wildlife Management Area
Off Rt. 607 north of Sunset Blvd.
Telephone: 609-628-2103
Hours: Dawn to dusk daily.
This one-and-a-half-mile stretch of beach also contains the last remnant of coastal dune forest on the bayshore. Higbee Beach is also known as a spectacular birding location. More than 250 species, including the bald eagle, frequent the beach. It is also home to dragonflies and butterflies, including the monarch butterfly.

Cape May National Wildlife Refuge
24 Kimbles Beach Rd.
Cape May Court House, NJ 08210-2078
Telephone: 609-463-0994
Fax: 609-463-1667
E-mail: capemay@fws.gov
Hours: Dawn to dusk daily.
Established in January 1989, the Cape May National Wildlife Refuge is one of the newest national refuges. Besides supporting over 300 bird species, the Refuge is also home to snakes, frogs, and salamanders, some of them endangered species.

Tours and Shopping

Cape May provides tours not only for a variety of interests, but also with different modes of transportation. You can walk, ride a trolley, or even take a cruise to participate in some of the area's many activities, which include learning about the history of some of the houses, hearing ghost stories, or even sampling some of the region's finest wines.

Shopping in Cape May is equally versatile. You can look for collectibles, holiday decorations, funky nostalgia, crazy clothing, cooking gadgets, or homemade soap. Shopping in Cape May is basically concentrated at the Washington Street Mall; Washington Commons, across Washington Street from the mall; and Carpenter's Square Mall, behind the Washington Street Mall on Carpenter's Lane. There are also stores across from the beachfront on Beach Drive.

MAC tours usually start in one of two places: the MAC Information Booth, a kiosk on the Washington Street Mall, or the shiny red and green Mac trolley, which is enclosed and holds thirty to forty people. First purchase your tour tickets at the MAC kiosk, unless you've ordered ahead.

Wide and shady, the Washington Street pedestrian mall provides a unique shopping experience.
PAT KING-ROBERTS

The MAC kiosk is a modest structure that sits on the Washington Street side of the mall, across from the Star of the Sea church. Yet it is from here that tickets, maps, tour lists, brochures, and copious amounts of other information come flowing forth like water from a faucet. The friendly MAC staffers inside the kiosk cheerfully answer each and every question, even though you know they've heard some of them a million times. Thus the MAC kiosk is actually one of Cape May's most important structures!

MAC often has special online coupons to save you money on many of these tours. They also send out monthly electronic newsletters that contain discount coupons on many Cape May activities. Go to the MAC website (www.capemay mac.org) to sign up and find out more information, or call 609-884-5404 or 800-275-4278.

GHOSTS OF CAPE MAY TOUR

Ah, ghosts. You can deny them or believe in them, but one thing is certain: Ghosts are a part of our popular culture through stories, TV, and movies.

No matter what your feeling is about ghosts, there certainly seems to be *something* out of the ordinary in Cape May. Perhaps it's the age of many of the buildings, or perhaps it's the town's proximity to water, both of which are supposed to attract spirits. Whatever it is, if you're walking down a dark street in Cape May at night, and you feel like you're not alone . . . perhaps you're not.

"Cape May is a hotbed of paranormal activity," says psychic medium Craig McManus, who knows the town well. "Cape May has an energy to it. I'm not quite sure what the energy is, but it's definitely there."

McManus has written a book called *The Ghosts of Cape May*, available via his website or throughout Cape May. He is also the author of the popular Ghosts of Cape May trolley tour run by MAC. The tour goes through the Historic District, describing ghostly phenomena that have occurred there. It is spooky, amusing, and intriguing, all at once.

Cape May has a "positive energy," according to McManus, that begins once you cross over the Cape May bridge and get into the city. He estimates that as many as 60 percent of the old buildings in Cape May are haunted. "There's too much evidence to deny that something paranormal is happening there," he says, adding that this amount of supernatural activity is usually seen on battlefields or other scenes of tragedy, but not in a resort town.

He believes that one reason Cape May has so many ghosts is the same reason why we mortals venture to the Jersey Shore: fondness. After all, he points out, ghosts are nothing more than energy with a brain, and their brain points them to the same places that mortals go. He also says that ghosts dislike crowds as much as we do. That's why ghostly activity tends to decline in the summer, when the town is filled with hordes of tourists. It's also the reason why so much ghostly activity occurs in attics. Ghosts are just trying to get away from it all in the house, and the attic is one of the least crowded places.

Unfortunately for fertile imaginations and Hollywood screenwriters, McManus says that 99 percent of all hauntings tend to be benign. But that doesn't mean ghostly encounters can't be scary. He tells of a couple staying in an inn in Cape May who kept hearing footsteps running up and down the stairs, followed by a rap on their door. Tiring of this, the man decided to confront the culprit. The next time he heard footsteps, he yanked open the door. Facing him was–nothing. The entire landing was deserted. Suddenly he felt a blast of very cold air. He calmly closed and locked the door. Then he and his wife packed their suitcases and left by climbing through the window and dropping onto the front porch . . . anything to avoid that landing.

McManus had a frightening experience of his own. He was lying in bed in Cape May when the covers were pulled down, and he felt someone . . . something . . . crawl into bed next to him. He felt the mattress depress but didn't want to turn and see what was lying next to him. Eventually whatever it was got up and left.

"Now that was scary," he says.

Yup.

The Ghosts of Cape May Tour is sponsored by MAC. It's held at night (naturally) and uses the distinctive red and green MAC trolley. The tour begins on Ocean Street, which is where the trolley always loads and unloads. Ocean Street is the road directly across from the Washington Street Mall, on the side by the MAC kiosk and the Star of the Sea church. When it's awaiting passengers, the trolley is always parked on Ocean Street, almost directly across from the MAC kiosk.

After it's loaded, the trolley wastes little time in getting to the Historic District, where it seems that 99.99 percent of all Cape May's paranormal activity occurs. Then it slowly meanders up and down the streets of the district, as a MAC guide weaves ghost stories based on the findings of Craig McManus.

Sometimes the stories are directly related to a house–a figure is often seen peeking out of a third-floor window, or an unseen ghost gently rocks back and forth in the rocking chairs on a front porch. Other times, the stories take on a more indistinct quality, such as one about the old man in very proper nineteenth-century dress who can be seen twirling his cane and sauntering down the street in night's gloom . . . until you come closer, at which point he vanishes. Sometimes animals get into the act too, such as the ghostly horse-drawn carriage that can occasionally be heard clopping up and down historic Jackson Street . . . heard, that is, but never seen.

In the darkness, as the trolley glides through the streets and the guide's voice wraps around you as he or she relates these tales of spooky encounters, the ride takes on an eerie, almost surreal quality. You could almost be a phantom yourself, floating through the misty streets of Cape May with their large trees looming up along the sidewalk like silent sentinels in some supernatural dimension. The Victorian houses, so much a part of another time and place, add to the atmosphere, particularly since some are outlined in white light, which just adds to the unworldly feeling.

The tour takes about forty-five minutes and lets you back off at the MAC trolley loading-unloading area on the brightly lit Ocean Street. Then, for some, it's a several-block walk back to the B&B down the same dark streets that the tour just went through. That's when the true test of whether or not a person believes in ghosts kicks in!

WINERY CELLAR TOUR AND TASTING

Cape May Winery and Vineyard recently opened a new 5,000-square-foot production facility, tasting room, and sales shop. This is all the more reason to take the Cape May Winery Cellar Tour and Tasting.

The Cape May Winery is one of New Jersey's southernmost wineries. Its proximity to both the Atlantic Ocean and Delaware Bay enables it to experience more moderate winters, which means a longer growing season for grapes. This allows the winery to grow vinifera grapes for such wines as Chardonnay, Riesling, and Merlot. Genial winemaker Darren Hesington explains all this and more on a delightful tour of the winery, including the vineyards and production facilities.

Although the winery's wines have won numerous awards in statewide competition, and are obviously major players in a burgeoning New Jersey wine industry, Hesington does not take himself too seriously. His jokes and lighthearted humor liven up what otherwise could be a dry, technical treatise on how wine is made. He patiently fields all questions and gives detailed answers, especially when the tour group contains people who make their own wines at home and press him for specific information.

The tour starts outside the winery, in front of rows and rows of grapevines gently wafting in the wind. Here Hesington talks about many of the technical aspects of growing certain types of grapes, how long the growing season has to be, soil consistency, trimming and shaping the vines so that they don't get out of control, and

From grapevines such as these come some of New Jersey's finest wines. MID-ATLANTIC CENTER FOR THE ARTS

Cape May's milder winter temperatures significantly aid the grape-growing effort. MID-ATLANTIC CENTER FOR THE ARTS

how diligent he and the entire staff must be against frost, which can wipe out a grape harvest. From there the tour moves inside to the room where the wine is processed and bottled.

But the highlight of the tour is the wine tasting. Here the winery goes all out to please its guests. The number of wines tasted is very large, and they run the gamut from very dry to very sweet. Each is introduced by Hesington, who gives a little speech about the wine's history from grape to bottle, and whether it came out the way he wanted. It makes you realize that despite all the technical advances, wine making is still an extremely inexact science.

Accompanying the wine is a hefty plate of various cheeses. That, and the generous amounts of each wine sampled, means that if you take this tour in the afternoon, you're going to have a hard time finishing your dinner. By the time you've tasted all the wines that are offered, you'll end this tour feeling better than you did at the beginning!

The winery is located in nearby Lower Township, at 709 Townbank Road. No transportation is provided from Cape May. You have to drive to it yourself. Allow fifteen to twenty minutes to reach the winery from the center of town.

AROUND CAPE ISLAND HISTORY CIRCLE TOUR

At some point aboard the *Cape May Whale Watcher* during the informative and relaxing Around Cape Island History Circle Tour, you're almost assured of seeing bottle-nosed dolphins pop their distinctive snouts out of the water. That's because, the captain explains, the dolphins have become so used to the familiar sounds of the boat and his voice that they recognize them and surface to say hi to this non-threatening vessel.

Dolphin sightings are just one of the many enjoyable aspects of the Around Cape Island tour, cosponsored by MAC. On the two-hour tour, the boat steams all around Cape May as far north as Wildwood. Along the way, the 110-foot clean and comfortable *Cape May Whale Watcher* passes over the submerged foundations of an old residential area, past the slowly sinking remnants of the concrete ship, and along the coast where the Cape May Lighthouse beams. The tour even includes neighboring Wildwood. The captain explains and describes all the sights in an informative and frequently humorous narration with a mix of history and current events. Such things as the concrete ship, lighthouse, various houses and sites on land (such as the location of Cape May's former nude beach . . . but that's a topic for a different book), and even the construction of bridges and canals are covered in the extensive narration.

The *Cape May Whale Watcher* is an extremely large and easy-riding boat that offers seating both on top, under the sun and sky, and below, with a protective roof. It also features a long area jutting out from the front of the boat, called a pulpit, on which you can wander, if you don't mind a little saltwater spray in your face. As you can imagine, it is an ideal location from which to spot marine life. Underneath your feet is nothing but ocean water. The ship has a snack bar in case the munchies strike and separate male and female bathrooms.

During the voyage, it's likely that a dolphin, porpoise, or even a whale may show up to greet you and the boat. Sightings of marine mammals are so frequent that the *Cape May Whale Watcher* offers a guarantee: If you don't see a marine mammal, you receive a free pass for another trip. A crew of naturalists offer tips on marine sightings during the cruise. Once an animal is seen, they are able to almost predict its movements and how often it'll stay surfaced for frantically picture-snapping tourists. Turns out that some of the crew members have seen these animals so often that they can actually recognize individual ones.

The dolphins and porpoises seem to have the most fun with the boat. They frequently ride in the wake and leap out of it occasionally like salmon heading upstream. The camera-ready visitor with a telephoto lens can get sensational pictures.

The *Cape May Whale Watcher* is a familiar sight in the waters around Cape May. PAT KING-ROBERTS

The tour is a wonderfully refreshing activity on a hot summer day. Out on the water, as the boat cuts through the open sea, your cares and worries will disappear as the heat of the mainland dissolves into the salty spray.

The *Cape May Whale Watcher* offers a selection of other trips as well, such as a sunset dolphin watch and a fireworks cruise. The Miss Chris Marina, where the trips originate, was slated to be developed several years ago, until the captain and others fought back and ultimately purchased it to save it from development. Good thing.

Several other whale- and dolphin-watching cruises are also offered in Cape May. You'll find the *Cape May Whale Watcher* at the Miss Chris Marina, which is located at the first right turn after you cross the large bridge entering Cape May. Parking is extremely limited. The marina does have a lot, but depending on the time of your cruise, it may be filled with the cars of passengers of the previous cruise, and there is no street parking. So parking is a matter of timing and luck. For information on cruises and rates, call 800-786-5445 or 609-884-5445, or log on to www.capemay whalewatcher.com. The boat is wheelchair accessible with some limitations.

DISCOVER CAPE MAY HISTORIC HOUSE TOUR

This is the perfect tour for those just getting familiar with Cape May. It is a self-guided walking tour that allows you to wander all through the Historic District at your own pace, visiting more than a dozen Victorian homes. At each one, the innkeeper or owner answers questions about everything from the wallpaper to the flowers in the garden. Charming, genial, and informative, many put out refreshments for their foot-weary visitors and let them relax on the rocking chairs or settees on the front porch.

Pick up a list and map of the houses on the tour at the MAC kiosk on the Washington Street Mall, across from the Star of the Sea church. From there it's about three short blocks to the beginning of the Historic District. You then have to rely on the map to find your way around the district. It's a good way to get to know the area, seeing as how it's a rabbit warren of small and one-way streets.

Walking through the Historic District is a very pleasant jaunt indeed. The streets, lined with classic Victorian structures, are shady and cool. Many have flower gardens exploding in a riot of color. Walking through the district at your own pace allows you to examine the houses' architectural details, admire the gardens, and drink in the atmosphere of this beautiful area.

Another benefit of walking the district is the people you'll meet and the friends you'll make. It starts at the MAC kiosk, where fate just happens to throw together a random group of strangers who have an interest in wandering through Cape May. It continues at each house, where you can ask as many questions of the owner or innkeeper as you like. Since you're not part of a set group, people come and go, meet up and part, in a completely random pattern.

There's something totally refreshing about wandering the streets at a leisurely pace, stopping in at the various houses along the tour. It evokes memories of times past, when on New Year's Day the Dutch settlers of early New York City would visit each other's homes.

Victorian house tours let visitors in on the history of Cape May. MID-ATLANTIC CENTER FOR THE ARTS

OTHER NOTABLE MAC TOURS

MAC offers dozens of tours, each with its own unique theme, and new ones are added to the list all the time. Call 609-884-5404 or 800-275-4278 for further information. You can also get on a list to receive a MAC newsletter that talks about upcoming events and tours. Some MAC tours are offered year-round, whereas others are just given in certain seasons. Some tours tend to sell out very quickly, but others still have spaces open on the day of the tour. There's really no way to predict which will be available and which will not. The best way to make sure you get to go on the tour you want is to reserve tickets in advance. The following are some of the other MAC tours.

Historic Beachfront Tour

Climb aboard the MAC trolley to hear about how the beachfront developed from the Victorian era up through the present day.

Cape May Sampler Tour

This introductory tour of four of Cape May's most famous Victorian bed-and-breakfast inns and guesthouses will help you find out what the city is all about. At each location, the innkeeper tells about the building's restoration, the decorating scheme, and more. At the conclusion, the MAC trolley takes you to the Carriage House Tearoom for tea and a sampling of sweets, including tea breads, scones, cookies, chocolate, and fruit.

Audio Walking Tour of Cape May's Historic District

This self-guided walking tour is another great introduction to Cape May. For this tour, you get a taped narration in addition to a map and index for ninety-six historic buildings at sixty-eight sites. The narration describes some history as well as the various architectural styles you encounter.

Family Treasure Hunt Tour of Cape May

This is a good way to get the kids involved in the whole Cape May experience, and a sneaky way to perhaps teach them something about the area. Pick up a Treasure Hunt packet at the Washington Street Mall Information Booth. It includes a map, clue sheet, and answer sheet. Then you and the kids wander the streets on a scavenger hunt, trying to find items in response to the clues.

Fisherman's Wharf Tour

This guided tour of Fisherman's Wharf at the Lobster House restaurant dock traces the journey of fish from sea to dinner table. Does it surprise you to learn that Cape May is the second-largest commercial fishing port on the East Coast? Find out how and why here. The tour is offered from June through August.

Natural Habitats Tour

This tour is a primer for nature lovers, as it details the natural habitats and attractions that have made Cape May a must-stop for those who want to get away from it all.

World War II Trolley Tour

Cape May played an interesting role in World War II. Fort Miles, a complex of coastal batteries and observation towers built in 1941 by the U.S. Army to guard the mouth of the Delaware Bay, was the most highly fortified location per acre in America. When an erroneous *Time* magazine article reported that Cape May's beaches were full of barbed wire and oil slicks, it crippled the city's tourist trade. The city countered with a campaign titled "V is for Victory and Vacations," emphasizing the importance of traveling for good morale.

During the war, the city's Admiral Hotel was taken over by the U.S. Navy. The main floor was occupied by the Joint Operations Delaware Group, while the upper floors served as the bachelor officers quarters (BOQ).

There were constant rumors that German spies and saboteurs were landing in the area, but no definitive evidence of such was ever found.

On the World War II Trolley Tour, you visit some of the key sites during the war, such as a magnesite plant, the Cape May Canal, the Admiral Hotel, and Naval Air Station Wildwood. The tour will give you a greater appreciation of the role the area played in the war.

WASHINGTON STREET MALL

Although there are shops galore in Cape May, nowhere are they better clustered or easier to get to than at the Washington Street outdoor pedestrian shopping mall. The term *mall* in this case does not mean an enclosed glass and steel edifice anchored by giant retail stores. Rather, it's an example of the second definition of the word: an urban street lined with shops and closed off to motor vehicles.

Large and wide, the mall runs for three blocks, from Ocean Street to Perry Street. It has nearly fifty stores offering everything from antiques to clothing to Christmas items to gifts as well as a number of restaurants. It's the focal point of Cape May and a common point of reference, with many establishments giving their location in terms of how many blocks they are from the Washington Street Mall.

The mall also contains, on the Ocean Street side, the MAC Kiosk Information Booth, a kiosk where you can get tour information, purchase tour tickets, and find out practically anything else about Cape May activities. Rest assured that you'll find yourself stopping here often.

No matter the season, the Washington Street Mall ranks among Cape May's can't-miss attractions.
PAT KING-ROBERTS

Visiting Cape May is like taking a trip back in time, and nowhere is this more evident than at the mall. Just the lack of cars alone makes this a unique experience. You can wander from one side of the mall to the other as your heart desires and your window-shopping eyes command.

The mall is beautifully landscaped with trees and flowers. It is also gaily decorated for the Christmas season, and it is not unusual to encounter roving groups of musicians or performers at any time during the peak seasons. It has numerous benches, so you can usually find a place to relax when needed. A large listing of stores is prominently displayed at each end. Comfort stations are located across the street from the Star of the Sea church, in Washington Commons, near where the horses and carriages line up.

Many of the mall's stores have been in the same family for generations. This is not a place to find chains or trendy outlet stores. But if you like stores where you can talk to knowledgeable salespeople who may also be the owners, this is your kind of place. Privately owned shops with the owners working in them have a homey feeling and recall the days before big-box behemoths, when service and chatting with the person behind the cash register were both helpful and a pleasure, and part of the overall shopping experience.

Take time to explore the little side alleys. Liberty Way, for example, just a few feet down from the Star of the Sea church, has almost a dozen stores selling a variety of merchandise. These and the other alleys are well worth the shoe leather.

One of the best things to do at the mall in nice weather is to eat outside at one of its numerous restaurants. Get there early in peak times or be prepared to wait. There is nothing nicer than dining outside as the sun sets, the cool night breezes emerge, and you reflect on your Cape May day.

The only hassle about the Washington Street Mall is parking. During busy seasons, such as midsummer and Christmas, trying to find a spot near the mall is like trying to find the proverbial needle in the haystack. There are metered spots on the alleys alongside the mall, Carpenter's Lane and Lyle Lane, but to find one you have to be in great favor with the Parking Gods. You can park in the Acme parking lot across the street from Ocean Street, a gated lot that charges a fee during peak seasons.

At such times, your best bet is to leave your car wherever you're staying and simply walk to the mall. Even if it's several blocks away, Cape May blocks are small, and before you know it you'll be at the mall. It's just about three blocks from the Historic District, so you can be at the mall in no time. And when you consider the benefits of being able to leisurely stroll the mall rather than having to watch the time because you're parked at a meter, the choice becomes obvious.

Christmas season is a fun time to visit. On Friday and Saturday nights of the second weekend in December, the Washington Street Mall hosts Hospitality Night. Mall merchants put out food and drink, and everyone has a blast wandering in and out of stores, eating, drinking, conversing with the shopkeepers, and buying. This is an event not to be missed.

During peak seasons, mall stores are open long hours daily, often until 10 P.M. Because they are privately owned, many open and close at their owners' discretion during the off-season, and hours can be erratic then. In January or February, a store might not open for days if the weather's nasty and the owner figures nobody's

Winterwood on the pedestrian mall, where it's
Christmas every day of the year. PAT KING-ROBERTS

going to be out on the mall. If you plan
to visit during the off-season, call or
check a store's website to find out if it
will be open when you arrive.

Following are descriptions of a few
of the many stores of the Washington
Street Mall.

Winterwood Gift and Christmas Gallery

If you like holidays, particularly Christmas, once you enter Winterwood, you're
not going to want to leave. As it advertises, Winterwood is a gift and Christmas
gift shop, but the emphasis is heavily on
Christmas ornaments of all shapes and
sizes. You can find a wide array of decor
for your Christmas tree, including deli-
cate glass ornaments, tiny crabs and lob-
sters with Santa hats, and Cape May
historic homes. Suffice it to say that if
you can't find something you want to buy for your tree, you just aren't trying.

But there's more . . . lots more. Do you need strings of indoor Christmas lights?
Winterwood's got them. Are you looking for collectible Santa Claus figures with
the jolly fat man in golf clothes or a Hawaiian shirt? Winterwood's got them. How
about cloth figures in full caroling voice? Winterwood's got them.

Winterwood has plenty of Halloween items too, such as haunted houses,
ceramic witches, pumpkins, and monsters. For St. Patrick's Day, the store offers a
selection of Celtic-oriented figures to celebrate the wearing of the green. Winterwood also has a great selection of gifts, such as Cat's Meow Cape May houses.

Visiting Winterwood

518 Washington Street Mall, Cape May, NJ 08204
Telephone: 609-884-8949
Website: www.winterwoodgift.com

Hours: June 1 through Labor Day, daily, 10 A.M. to 10 P.M.; remainder of year,
daily, 10 A.M. to 5 P.M. Call to check on extended hours.
Credits cards: All major credit cards accepted.
Personal checks: Not accepted.

For many years, Winterwood was located at 526 Washington Street Mall. There was a lot of talk that the store was haunted, with stories about things mysteriously falling from shelves. At the end of 2005, Winterwood moved just a few stores down, to its current corner location in a former bank building. No word yet on whether any ghosts came along for the ride. Disappointed spirit seekers will have to be content with the Winterwood store in the historic Hildreth House on Route 9 in nearby Rio Grande, which is thought to be so haunted that there's a sign explaining it outside.

But even without the ghosts, Winterwood is a great place to explore. If you are a Christmas junkie, this is where you'd want to spend eternity.

Donna's Hallmark Shop

So if you were owner Steve Protasi, how would you turn your card store into more than just a card store? Simple. You would make it a destination for collectors of all types of figurines.

Of course, you'll find greeting cards here. They come in all shapes and sizes, and range from the bawdy to the musical. Because there are no big-box retailers or chain drugstores in Cape May, Donna's is one of the few places to get a greeting card for any occasion.

But it's more than just cards that makes Donna's such a great place. Protasi has stocked the store with such an incredible selection of high-end collectibles that going there is simply a treat for collectors who have to scratch that collecting itch even while in Cape May.

Donna's Hallmark has a wide selection of Hummel figurines and the hard-to-find Spoontique Lighthouses, all of them displayed. In addition, the store also carries gorgeous items—made by local talent—that are right up there in quality with the national collections. For example, there was a selection of wonderful, detail-specific lighthouse statues by a local artist until she moved away. Her Hereford Inlet Lighthouse (in Wildwood) even depicted the structure's famous gardens, with individual colored flowers. Now that's detail.

You can find some unusual things here as well, such as ceiling fan pulls, clown figures, gremlins, and other small statues. But that's Donna's Hallmark—collectibles and a lot of things you won't find anywhere else. Instead of being a typical card store, Donna's is more like a toy store for grown-ups.

Visiting Donna's Hallmark

401 Washington Street Mall, Cape May, NJ 08204
Telephone: 609-884-0555
Email: cmdonna21@hotmail.com

Hours: In-season, daily, 10 A.M. to 11 P.M.; off-season, daily, 11 A.M. to 5 P.M.
   Call to verify precise seasonal hours.
Credit cards: MasterCard, Visa, and Discover.
Personal checks: Not accepted.

Visiting the Original Fudge Kitchen

513 Washington Street Mall, Cape May, NJ 08204
Telephone: 800-23-FUDGE
Website: www.fudgekitchens.com

Hours: Summer, 9 A.M. to 11 P.M. daily; winter, weekdays, 9 A.M. to 6 P.M.; weekends, 9 A.M. to 8 P.M. Call to check on extended hours.
Credit cards: MasterCard and Visa.
Personal checks: Accepted.

The Original Fudge Kitchen

They're out there in the summer, fall, spring, and winter. They're out there in the morning . . . oh heck, they're seemingly out there *all* the time. You can usually find Original Fudge Kitchen employees standing outside the store nearly any time of day, offering free samples of their incredibly good confection.

At first you try to ignore them. After all, it wouldn't be appropriate for you to give in to your sweet tooth and devour every sample in their basket. But then your willpower starts to falter, and you politely take a sample with a smile. Once you taste it, you're doomed. In a few moments, you find yourself back there, taking another sample out of the basket while doing your best Homer Simpson drool.

Then you notice that they're whipping the fudge right in the front window of the store. You can actually see them preparing another scrumptious batch in front of your eyes. At this point, you can't resist going inside, where the delicious chocolate smells overtake you, so you buy some fudge. Several pounds of the different flavors. Then, as long as you're there, maybe you should try some of the other great candy, such as coconut clusters, chocolate truffles, malt balls . . .

The Original Fudge Kitchen has been a Cape May must-stop for more than three decades. And just in case you're on the Cape May beach and you suddenly get an irresistible craving for fudge, there's also a store at 728 Beach Avenue, near Convention Hall on the Promenade.

Whale's Tale

There are many gift shops in Cape May. This is simply one of the best.

Do you need a deck of playing cards in the shape of dog bones? How about a kit to send your own message in a bottle? Or maybe a tape dispenser in the shape of a frog? If you do, the Whale's Tale has got you covered. For more than thirty years, the Whale's Tale has been selling things that simply can't be found elsewhere from a red brick building in front of the four-sided clock on the mall.

One thing that's fun to shop for at the Whale's Tale is jewelry. This is not typical jewelry. Like everything that finds its way into the store, the jewelry at the Whale's Tale is unique. If you're looking for a pin in the shape of a jellyfish, look no farther. If you're a big horseshoe crab fan and want a horseshoe crab neck-

Visiting the Whale's Tale

312 Washington Street Mall, Cape May NJ 08204
Telephone: 609-884-4808
Fax: 609-884-1320
Website: www.whalestalecapemay.com
E-mail: info@whalestalecapemay.com

Hours: Summer, 10 A.M. to 11 P.M.; winter, 10 A.M. to 5 P.M.
Credit cards: Accepted.
Personal checks: Accepted.

lace, it's here. Or maybe you'd like earrings in the shape of blue crabs. They're here as well.

Besides odd and unusual gifts, the Whale's Tale carries books and cards, and it hasn't forgotten the smaller set either. There are plenty of things that a child can find amusing here, such as those crazy Russian nesting dolls, toys, puzzles, and bizarre-looking seashells.

Allow plenty of time to browse through the Whale's Tale, and come back to check out all those things that you missed the first time. But be warned: Somebody else has her eye on that bright orange clown fish mobile.

A Place on Earth

A Place on Earth is simply like no other place on Earth. The first thing you notice is the wonderful smells. Cinnamon, lemon, lavender, rose, tangerine, coconut, strawberry, and a hundred other fragrances greet you when you enter the shop, which is below the Winterwood store. That's because they're all part of the ingredients of the store's soaps, bath salts, and other wildly inventive products, such as tub teas—giant tea bags full of dried herbs.

All of the soaps at A Place on Earth are hand-stirred, cured in wooden molds, and hand-cut, just like they used to be way back when. But what really makes A Place on Earth unique is that only plant life and other vegetable-based ingredients are used in its products. Things like ground oats, cornmeal, and oils of olive, coconut, and palm. Organic botanicals, such as lavender flowers and rosemary, are

Visiting A Place on Earth

525 Washington Street Mall, Cape May, NJ 08204
Telephone: 866-400-SOAP
Website: www.aplaceonearth.com

Hours: Summer, daily, 10 A.M. to 10 P.M.; Winter, daily, 10:30 A.M. to 5 P.M.
Credit cards: Visa, MasterCard, and American Express.
Personal checks: Not accepted.

A Place on Earth carries a bounty of fragrant, handmade bath products. PAT KING-ROBERTS

mixed in. Then every product is tested on friends, family, and other willing human guinea pigs—not on helpless laboratory animals.

The results are some of the most inventive soap and bath products since the invention of the bathtub. Try finding soaps named Patchouli Love Bar, Cuban Mojito Bar, and Fresh Cut Grass Bar at your local supermarket. Or look for a bath scrub called Sex on the Beach. All of the scrubs here are made with sugar instead of salt, because sugar is kinder and gentler to the body. And you know those annoying places, like on the back of your heel, where the skin always seems rough and flaky? There are special products for those areas too.

A Place on Earth was formerly located in a strip mall in West Cape May. In 2006, it moved to this new location at the Washington Street Mall, just below Winterwood. No matter where it is, it's still one of the best places on earth.

CITY CENTRE MALL

In the middle of the Washington Street Mall is a large building that looks like any other storefront but in truth houses . . . another mall. It's a mini-mall called the City Centre Mall, with about a dozen stores spread over two floors. A convenient escalator goes to the second floor, but unfortunately there isn't one leading down, when you might be package-laden. Among the stores here is one dedicated to displaying the paintings of Thomas Kinkade. But perhaps the coolest store here is Marlene's Gifts.

Marlene's Gifts

If you're a nostalgia buff or a pop culture freak, or you just like really odd things, this is the store for you. Marlene, one of the biggest *Survivor* fans in the world, has assembled an amusing and interesting collection of pop-culture and entertainment items that you're not likely to run across anywhere else.

For instance, there are clocks here, but they're not just any clocks. No, some feature Betty Boop, some feature movie icons like King Kong, and some feature TV personalities like the Honeymooners. But that's not all. This isn't exactly the biggest store in the world, but it just might contain more merchandise per square inch than any other. You'll find figurines of the Marx Brothers, the Wizard of Oz stars, and other entertainment icons; posters of movies, both famous and obscure; bobble-head

---

Visiting Marlene's Gifts

City Centre Mall, 421 Washington Street, Cape May, NJ 08204
Telephone: 609-884-0706

Hours: Summer, 10 A.M. to 11 P.M.; winter, daily, 10 A.M. to 5 P.M.
Credit cards: All major credit cards accepted.
Personal checks: Not accepted.

---

figures of celebrities; movie star mugs; crazy key chains. Pretty much anything that you can't imagine would be in a store, you'll find here. Call it pop-culture kingdom.

And then there's Marlene, the genial host of all this madness. She never seems too busy to engage you in a *Survivor* chat and somehow knows exactly where everything is in the store. Marlene's Gifts is a great place to explore.

OTHER SHOPPING

Cape May has a lot of great stores. To name them all would constitute a book unto itself. Below is just a sampling of the interesting stores you can find, including MAC's shop at the Emlen Physick House.

Carriage House Gallery Shop

Anyone for tea? That's what will come to your mind when you enter this MAC store in the Carriage House on the Emlen Physick Estate. Just past the shop is the Carriage House Tearoom, and it makes sense to devote a shop to all things tea right next to it.

And the phrase "all things tea" is no exaggeration. Do you need a teapot? Cup? Saucer? Stirring spoon? Sugar bowl? Tea bag caddy? They're all here. But that's just getting started. There are also books about tea, holiday ornaments for your tree in the shape of cups and tea bags, collectible teapots, and wall-mounted racks for you to display all of your teacups at home. For the child planning to host tea parties, there are kids' tea sets. There's also a complete selection of Twinings teas, including raspberry, peppermint, black currant, mango, and dozens of others.

It's always tea time at MAC's Carriage House Gallery Shop. MID-ATLANTIC CENTER FOR THE ARTS

Visiting the Carriage House Gallery Shop

Emlen Physick Estate, 1048 Washington St., Cape May, NJ 08204
Telephone: 609-884-5404 or 800-275-4278
Website: www.capemaymac.org

Hours: Monday through Saturday, 10 A.M. to 5 P.M., Sunday, 11 A.M. to 4 P.M.
Credit cards: All major credit cards accepted.
Personal checks: Accepted.

The store is not large, so the first impression when you walk in is something approaching an out-of-control tea riot. But time and a little patience will allow you to see all the items and make a selection that will be the envy of your tea-loving friends back home.

Oma's Doll Shop

315 Ocean Street, #5 Washington Commons, 609-884-8882 and 877 274-DOLL (3655), fax: 609-884-2717, www.omasdollshop.com

You want dolls? Oma's has close to 1,000 of them under one roof. You'll find collectible series, such as Little Souls, Show Stoppers, and Alexander dolls. You'll find dolls dressed in every conceivable style and fashion, from nurses and doctors to cheerleaders. The store even has an Adoption Center with infant dolls that are sculpted, dressed, jointed, and have the weight of a real newborn baby. They're in tiny cradles behind a window, just like newborns at a hospital nursery, and come with a birth certificate. The sign over the front window of the store reads, "Expectant Father's Waiting Room." Oma's is located in Washington Commons, the collection of shops across Washington Street from the pedestrian mall.

Cape May Beach and Kite Shop

1218 Route 109, 609-898-2022, www.cape maykites.com

Yes indeed, this is the store you saw when first coming into Cape May, with all those kites and windsocks out front turning crazily in the breeze. There are more kites in here than you could ever hope to find, including a farmer on a tractor and a bright yellow school bus. You'll also find kite accessories and items to enjoy on the beach, such as horseshoes, boogie boards, and beach chairs.

The Cape May Beach and Kite Shop carries all manner of kites, windsocks, and beach toys. PAT KING-ROBERTS

Celebrate Cape May

315 Ocean Street, 609-884-9032, www.celebratecapemay.com

This store offers everything you could ever want having to do with Cape May, and lots of things you never thought you wanted but can't really pass up once you see them. If it's about Cape May, it's here—clothing, pencils, lighthouses, glasses, piggy banks, mugs, magnets, ornaments, and a whole lot more.

Mother Grimm's Bears

727 Beach Drive, in the Macomber Hotel, 609-886-1200, www.mothergrimmsbears.com

You can't "bear" to miss this unusual store, which is run by a mother and daughter. Ellen Grimm began creating memory bears many years ago after she received an old fur coat from a friend. She combined her fond memories of her friend with her love for teddy bears to create the first Mother Grimm's Bear. Demand for the bears grew, and today she and her daughter Jennifer make teddy bears out of old fur pieces and garments that have special meaning to people.

WEST CAPE MAY TOUR AND SHOPPING

West Cape May is one of this area's best-kept secrets. Tourists who venture out of Cape May proper and toward the lighthouse or Cape May Point State Park are usually unaware that they have entered a new town. West Cape May begins approximately at Swain's Hardware. The distance from the center of Cape May to this location is less than half a mile. If it's a nice day and you feel like walking, West Cape May is just several blocks from the Washington Street Mall. You also can reach it easily by bicycle from the center of Cape May or the Historic District.

West Cape May has a fine selection of shops, restaurants, and B&Bs. Amazingly, the town does not have parking meters, which means if you're lucky enough to find a spot, you can park and explore without having to worry about the time. Like Cape May, West Cape May does not have a typical downtown. Its stores and restaurants are mainly spread along three major roadways: Park Boulevard, Broadway, and Sunset Boulevard.

If you like antiquing, West Cape May is the place for you. It has numerous antique shops, with timeless treasures and timely bargains. It boasts numerous specialty stores too, such as Tea by the Sea, devoted to tea drinkers; the Bird House of Cape May, for backyard birding enthusiasts; and Weddings by the Sea, for those with upcoming nuptials.

West Cape May also has several fine-dining establishments, such as the Black Duck and Vanthia's Restaurant. But perhaps the most outstanding thing about the town is its festivals. West Cape May runs three major festival events: the Strawberry Festival, the Lima Bean Festival, and the Christmas Parade. The festivals take place at Wilbraham Park, which is located on West Perry and Broadway, at the beginning of West Cape May as you approach it from Cape May proper. The park is not very big—just about a block long and a block wide—and it's really just a green shady area

The MAC trolley is a convenient way to experience the sights and sounds of West Cape May. MID-ATLANTIC CENTER FOR THE ARTS

rather than a classic park, but it's often the center of the town's activities. It has a few benches and picnic tables, however, and is a nice place to sit.

Of the three festivals, the Lima Bean Festival, a unique event devoted to this green vegetable, stands out. Growing lima beans used to be a major source of income for West Cape May farmers, and this heritage is remembered at the festival, usually held in October. Wilbraham Park and the surrounding streets are jam-packed with people, all celebrating the lima. Everywhere you look, you see people with hats and T-shirts announcing their lima love. One of the town's clothing stores, Flying Fish Studios, produces clothing specifically for the festival, such as shirts saying "Sub-Lima." Held in the autumn, after the hordes of summer tourists have gone and before the Christmas crowds descend, the Lima Bean Festival is the perfect way to spend a pleasant autumn Saturday.

Of course, you can eat limas here as well. This may be the only place to get barbecued lima beans, lima bean chili, and a local favorite, lima bean cake. Yes, it's an acquired taste. A Lima Bean Festival king and queen, usually a cute toddler boy and girl, are crowned. You'll also find crafts, music, and a recipe contest featuring—what else—the lima bean. Everywhere there are baskets of lima beans, reminding one and all of why they've all come together in the first place for a fun, goofy time.

West Cape May Trolley Tour

Although MAC's West Cape May Trolley Tour does not contain a single lima bean, the tour takes visitors all through West Cape May, allowing you to see much of the town for yourself. The forty-five-minute tour focuses mostly on history and heritage, although some current information is included.

West Cape May, which was part of the old-time Cape Island, incorporated as a separate borough in 1884. The area was settled by a hodgepodge of groups, including *Mayflower* descendants, former slaves, riverboat pilots, and whalers. The trolley tour goes behind the scenes of the town to expand on some of its heritage with details you're not likely to find elsewhere.

Take the Sears and Roebuck houses, for instance. At the turn of the twentieth century, you could pick out a house from among certain styles in the Sears catalog, just like picking out a hammer or winter coat. The house would arrive unassembled in the mail, and then you'd put it together like a jigsaw puzzle. It's a mind-boggling concept, yet completely understandable in an age without a multitude of stores. The trolley tour goes past several of those homes still existing today in West Cape May, as the guide explains their history.

Another example of information you'll learn on the tour is about Goldbeater's Alley. Beating gold into a thickness of one-thousandth of an inch for use in gold leaf used to be quite an industry in West Cape May. The tour guide explains who did that chore and why.

The guide also informs visitors about the town's African-American heritage. Although there are no plaques or memorials describing their visits or where they went, some prominent blacks who have visited the area include George Washington Carver and Martin Luther King. Another who came to the Cape May area was the celebrated Harriet Tubman. She spent the summers from 1849 to 1852 in Cape May, working as a cook, scrubwoman, and laundress. Tubman used the money she earned to finance her trips into Maryland to bring more slaves to freedom in the North via the Underground Railroad.

Flying Fish Studio

Now for today's pop quiz: What does *Carpe Phaseolus Limensis* mean? Give up? It means "Seize the Lima." And that should tell you all you need to know about the wacky and creative West Cape May clothing store called Flying Fish Studio.

You know you're in for something unusual when you first pull up to the store. The front door is painted bright red, against a blue exterior, and standing nearby are a merman and mermaid. When you enter the store, a large, light brown dog ambles over. He smells you, then strolls back to his big pillow bed in the back.

But that's the way Flying Fish is. It's warm and homey, and it gives off a definite comfort vibe. The store is located in West Cape May, but thanks to the closeness of

---

Visiting Flying Fish Studio

130 Park Blvd., West Cape May, NJ 08204
Telephone: 609-884-2760 or 800-639-2085
Fax: 609-884-9295
Website: www.theflyingfishstudio.com
E-mail: questions@theflyingfishstudio.com

Hours: Summer, 10 A.M. to 6 P.M. daily; winter, Thursday through Sunday, 10 A.M. to 4 P.M., or by appointment.
Credit cards: Accepted.
Personal checks: Not accepted.

Unique clothing abounds at Flying Fish Studio, a funky shop along Park Boulevard. PAT KING-ROBERTS

the town to Cape May itself, Flying Fish is only a five- or ten-minute drive from the Cape May Historic District.

Flying Fish Studio is as wild and unpredictable as it gets. The store is the official creator of clothing for the Lima Bean Festival, and some of its clothing specifically relates to that. But what makes Flying Fish special is that the sayings aren't stamped out in a factory somewhere. Each phrase is thought up and executed by store owner Sue Lotozo and others, so that you're not going to run into the same phrases that seem to appear on T-shirts in every resort town. Now be honest: Where else can you get a shirt that says "Dalai Lima"?

But it isn't all lima beans here at Flying Fish. The rest of the clothing is just as inventive, thanks to the fact that Lotozo designs them all. Some are serene, like a picture of a giant egret looking for food among the cattails, with the Cape May Lighthouse in the distance. Some are wise, such as the shirt that says "Childhood Is a Journey, Not a Race." And some are zany, like the lima bean puns.

Besides clothing, Lotozo also uses her creative talents to design other funky and unique items, such as rugs, mugs, neckties, and jewelry. There's a definite comfort vibe here that your typical mall clothing store does not possess. Much of it comes from Lotozo. If you're fortunate enough to visit Flying Fish when she's there, she will talk and joke with you, particularly about some of the outrageous puns on the lima bean–oriented clothing. That's when you realize how Flying Fish got its name in the first place.

Come here for the clothes, and you'll want to stay for the warmth.

Bird House of Cape May

109 Sunset Boulevard, West Cape May, 609-898-8871 and 877-362-9200, www.bird houseofcapemay.com

For the birder who has everything, the Bird House is the ultimate store. Bird-feeders, birdbaths, birdhouses in all shapes, styles, and sizes . . . if it's about birds or birding, it's here. The store also carries other things, including nature-inspired gifts and items for the home.

Recreation, Leisure, and Performing Arts

There's so much to fill up your free time in Cape May. You can enjoy an after-dinner stage show or dine while watching the dolphins at sunset. You can keep active by bicycling, parasailing, fishing, or boating. You can relax with an aromatherapy massage or a stroll through an art gallery. Why not take advantage of all that Cape May has to offer?

FINE ARTS

Cape May has a fine art gallery. The Washington Commons Gallery on Ocean Street has a wide and varied collection of custom paintings by local, national, and international artists.

So you say you can't take a picture—all thumbs, no workable digits. Your finger constantly finds its way over the lens. All digital photography has meant to you is more and more chances to take lousy pictures. But you would dearly love to capture the quaintness and beauty of Cape May. What do you do? Relax. Patricia Rainey has got you covered.

Rainey is an artist who paints both local Cape May and other Jersey Shore scenes. Want an eye-catching representation of the Cape May Lighthouse for your wall? Rainey has one. How about a picture of the distinctive front of the Mad Batter Restaurant? Rainey has one of those too. What about something showing the picturesque buildings on Jackson Street? No problem.

What's all the more remarkable about her exquisite work is that she's never had a drawing lesson in her life. For those of us who can't even draw a lollipop tree, that hurts. "I just picked up a bunch of brushes and paints and started painting," she says.

Washington Commons Gallery

315 Ocean St., Cape May, NJ 08204
Telephone: 609-884-1880 • www.capemaygallery.com

Artist Patricia Rainey

North Cape May, NJ 08204
Telephone: 609-886-4863 • www.patriciaraineystudios.com

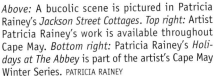

Above: A bucolic scene is pictured in Patricia Rainey's *Jackson Street Cottages. Top right:* Artist Patricia Rainey's work is available throughout Cape May. *Bottom right:* Patricia Rainey's *Holidays at The Abbey* is part of the artist's Cape May Winter Series. PATRICIA RAINEY

Rainey came to Cape May by way of New Hampshire and then North Jersey, where for years she ran a modeling agency. She came to Cape May to do some art shows, fell in love with the area, and decided to stay. One reason is that the sales season here is longer than in most other resort areas. "You can actually make a living as an artist," Rainey says.

Rainey mainly paints the numerous Cape May landmarks, but she will paint on commission. Her work, airy and light, captures the mood and feeling of this Victorian town without being muted or stodgy. It's as if the whole town is peeking out from under its Victorian lace and smiling.

"I paint happy because I feel that way," she says.

Rainey enjoys her relaxed life in Cape May, especially compared with the stressful world of professional modeling.

"I love it," she says with a smile. "Cape May is a real community. Everyone knows everyone."

Look for Rainey's work at Cape May's art galleries and at www.patriciarainey studios.com, as well as at local art shows. She estimates that she does shows twice a month from April through October.

THEATER

Cape May Stage is a professional equity theater company, featuring traditional, contemporary, and new works in an intimate setting. The group was founded in 1988. The following year it held its first performance, but didn't have a "home stage," so the shows took place at the historic Chalfonte Hotel and Cold Spring Village. Today the Cape May Stage hosts an ambitious and highly acclaimed eight-month schedule of six performances at its permanent home: a Renaissance Revival building built around 1853 that used to be a Presbyterian church. The theater seats about 110 people.

The season usually begins the week before Memorial Day in May. Each production lasts about a month, with breaks scattered throughout the schedule. Often a holiday-themed production ends the season, running from around Thanksgiving to just before Christmas.

The Cape May Stage theater is fully accessible to all persons with disabilities. It is equipped with a ramp to the front entrance and provides front-of-house seating for patrons with vision impairments or wheelchairs. Among the other disability-friendly features are wheelchair-accessible bathrooms, assisted-hearing devices, and large-print programs.

A popular way to enjoy a Cape May Stage production is with its Dinner and a

Show promotion, which partners the theater with some of the town's finest restaurants. Guests enjoy an early dinner at one of the eateries, then have the opportunity to purchase significantly reduced tickets for the 8 P.M. performance at Cape May Stage. Each restaurant runs its own individual special. Visit the Cape May Stage website for a list of participating restaurants. Some offer a special all-in-one price for dinner and a theater ticket; others offer a discounted ticket. All reservations must be made directly through the restaurant, not Cape May Stage.

In 2006, some of the Cape May restaurants that participated in this promotion were 410 Bank Street, the Ebbitt Room at the Virginia Hotel, and Tisha's Fine Dining. Although the roster of par-

The Cape May Stage puts on comedies and dramas in an intimate setting. CAPE MAY STAGE

The professional quality of Cape May Stage productions delights audiences year after year. CAPE MAY STAGE

ticipating restaurants may change yearly, Cape May's plethora of fine dining establishments means that there's always a great selection from which to choose.

The other Cape May theatrical group is the East Lynne Theater Company, which presents adaptations of American literature as well as American stage classics by authors such as Washington Irving, Steele McKaye, David Belasco, and Rachel Crothers. The company sometimes does other works as well. In 2006, for example,

Cape May Stage

Bank St. and Lafayette St. (theater location)
31 Perry St. (office)
Cape May, NJ 08204
Telephone: 609-884-1341• Fax: 609-884-4686
www.capemaystage.com

East Lynne Theater Company

First Presbyterian Church, 500 Hughes St. (theater location)
121 Fourth Ave. (office)
West Cape May, NJ 08204
Telephone: 609-884-5898• E-mail: Eastlynneco@aol.com
www.eastlynnetheater.org

it presented a play by a current Salt Lake City writer. The shows are held at the First Presbyterian Church.

The company's Cape May season starts around the third week of June and usually runs until about mid-December. Unlike the Cape May Stage productions, these plays usually run for just a very short period—four or five days—so the window of opportunity to see a show is very narrow.

These productions are completely accessible for those with special needs, and the company offers discount tickets to people with disabilities and their accompanying support companions. Other considerations for those with special needs include playbills available in large print and accessible seating for those with service animals. The theater also has an infrared audio amplification system.

Special events are featured throughout the season. One is Tales of the Victorians, in which a member of the company reads a classic American short story to guests on the front porch of a bed-and-breakfast while tea and treats are served. Numerous B&Bs take part. It's a great way to get into the spirit of Cape May!

The East Lynne Theater Company also has a special promotion including dinner at a Cape May restaurant along with a discounted performance ticket. In 2006, some of the participating restaurants were Althea's, the Mad Batter, and the Washington Inn. Check the theater company's website for more details, and call the individual restaurants to see what type of package they offer.

FISHING

Cape May is world renowned for its fishing. The Cape May Rips, located right where the Delaware Bay meets the Atlantic Ocean, is one of the best fishing spots in the world. And because Cape May is a coastal community, it also provides plenty of opportunity for surf fishers, who can pop up on any beach on the ocean or bay.

There's something both peaceful and life-affirming about watching surf fishers practicing the same skill that has been part of shore life for countless generations. With their poles stuck into the sand, fishing line extended into the sea, and gulls scampering about nearby, hoping for some wayward bait or food, surf fishers represent the continuity of tradition that is so much a part of coastal living. It seems that the more the world changes, and new developments and the latest technologies make their mark, the more peaceful and serene it feels to watch surf fishers challenge the sea, just as they have for centuries. The equipment may get fancier, but the basic struggle between human and fish remains.

A particularly popular site for surf fishers is Cape May Point State Park. Sometimes the beachfront here is lined with people trying their luck against their wily prey. From October through March, surf fishing is also allowed at the Cape May Wetlands Wildlife Management Area, Two Mile Beach Unit. Unless you immediately notice their fishing rods stuck into the sand, the surf fishers sitting in beach chairs peacefully reading or apparently dozing seem at first just like any other beachgoer seeking the ocean for relief from the summer heat. Cape May provides surf fishers opportunities at a wide variety of fish, including sharks, marlin, mackerel, and bluefish.

The waters off the Cape May coast offer ample opportunity for sport fishing. MID-ATLANTIC CENTER FOR THE ARTS

For those fishing from a boat, be warned that though the Cape May Rips is an excellent fishery, it is not a place for newcomers. It's an area of extremely strong currents, as might be expected in a place where two significant bodies of water are both fighting for the upper hand. Veteran anglers kid that they're not fishing close enough to catch fish if their boat does not hit bottom every once in a while at the Rips, but this kidding is said with respect, because the water in the Rips can go from twenty feet deep to two in the length of a small boat. For that reason, boats here are very susceptible to being swamped by an unexpectedly high wave. Unless you are a skilled fishing veteran, it's best not to fish the Rips without a guide. The ever-shifting bottom configurations and sudden water level changes can fool even the most confident angler. Although this fishery is best known for its blues, weak-fish, and striped bass, the continuous clash of two strong bodies of water means that one never quite knows what's to be found here.

As might be expected, there are numerous marinas in Cape May that are home base for party boats and charters.

Cape May Marinas

UTSCH'S MARINA
1121 Rt. 109, Cape May, NJ 08204 • Telephone: 609-884-2051

SOUTH JERSEY MARINA
1231 Rt. 109, Cape May, NJ 08204 • Telephone: 609-884-2400

CAPE MAY MARINE
1263 Lafayette St., Cape May, NJ 08204 • Telephone: 609-884-0262

MILL CREEK MARINA
Ocean Dr., Cape May, NJ 08204 • Telephone: 609-884-0065

BREE-ZEE-LEE YACHT BASIN
970 Ocean Dr., Cape May, NJ 08204 • Telephone: 609-884-4849

HINCH MARINA INC.
989 Ocean Dr., Cape May, NJ 08204 • Telephone: 609-884-7289

BICYCLING

If there is a better or more natural way to see Cape May or travel through it than by bicycle, it simply hasn't been invented yet. Because bicycling is so popular in Cape May, bicycles come in all shapes and sizes. There's the standard one-seater, bicycles built for two, and bicycles with little sidecars like motorcycles have for the seating of young children.

Some B&Bs and small hotels offer bicycles as a free service to their guests. Otherwise, you can bring your own or rent one. If you're getting the idea that Cape May is full of bicycles, you're right. They are simply all over, particularly in the busy spring and summer seasons, and it's the unwise visitor who does not first look both ways before entering a roadway or sidewalk . . . not for automobiles, but for bicycles.

To bicycle in Cape May is to enjoy the city at its finest. The first big benefit is that you won't have to hunt and pray for a parking spot, and then continually feed the voracious meter monster. The second is that you won't have any problem negotiating Cape May's narrow streets, made even tighter by the periodic horse-drawn carriage. A third benefit is that you can probably get to many places faster by biking than you can by car. In addition, there are no gas stations in the middle of town. The only place to fuel up your car is on the outskirts of Cape May coming into town.

But the major benefit of bicycling—and this is the big one—is that you are free to see and appreciate Cape May as it was meant to be seen and appreciated, in the open air. When you're biking, and not worrying about the myriad of things that driving demands, you can actually see that beautiful Victorian home with the red shutters and the wraparound porch . . . see it and admire it and think about how it must have been once to live there. Or you can stop in front of a house and admire its beautiful garden and gorgeous display of rose bushes. Perhaps more than any other town, Cape May is meant to be drunk in slowly, like a particularly fine glass of wine. Bicycling allows you to do just that.

Many of the streets in Cape May, such as Pittsburgh Avenue, have bicycle lanes. They cannot be beaten for safety and convenience, and they are widely used, especially in the summer.

Bicycling is a great way for the entire family to participate in an activity. Far too many people have the mistaken notion that Cape May is a one-dimensional place, where those not interested in all things Victorian need not bother to visit. But nothing could be further from the truth. Cape May is a great family vacation town, with a lot of activities for everyone to enjoy, including kids. Bicycling is one of those. Whether a child rides along behind a parent or is old enough to pedal his or her own bike, this is truly a family-oriented activity.

Fortunately, word seems to be getting out. Stroll around Cape May on any pleasant day in the spring, summer, or autumn, and you are likely to see dozens of bicycles tooling around the streets. The town abounds with bicycle racks, and it is quite common to see people bicycling to their favorite restaurant for coffee, the newspaper, or most anything else.

New Jersey state law requires riders under the age of seventeen to wear a helmet. It also requires bicycle passengers or anyone towed by a bicycle to also wear a

Cape May Bicycle Rentals

CAPE ISLAND BICYCLE CENTER
Three locations:
727 Beach Ave. (Beach and Howard Streets at the Hotel Macomber),
Cape May, NJ 08204
1100 block of New Jersey Ave. (behind the Buckingham Motel),
Cape May, NJ 08204
135 Sunset Blvd. (just before the Wicker Outlet),
West Cape May, NJ 08204

Telephone: 609-884-8011
Reservation office: 609-898-RENT (7368)

SHIELDS BIKE RENTALS
11 Guerney Ave., Cape May, NJ 08204
Telephone: 609-898-1818

VILLAGE BICYCLE SHOP
605 Lafayette St., Cape May, NJ 08204
Telephone: 609-884-8500

STECK'S BIKES
251 Beach Dr., Cape May, NJ 08204
Telephone: 609-884-1188

helmet. Be smart! This law is vigorously enforced, especially in Cape May, where bicycling is a primary mode of transportation. Don't think that you can just plop the kids on the back and make a quick run up the block to pick up a newspaper. Not only is this risky, but if you get caught—and you probably will—you will get ticketed. Don't take a chance. If you are uneasy about wearing a provided helmet, bring one from home. This helmet law also applies to roller skates, in-line skates, and skateboards.

Many lodging facilities provide bicycles for their guests to use. If yours does not, there are several places in Cape May to rent bicycles.

PARASAILING

Parasailing is an increasingly popular activity among those with an adventurous spirit. A boat pulls you while you soar aloft over the ocean, borne by a kitelike sail. All of the Cape May Parasail boat captains are certified by the U.S. Coast Guard.

Trips leave on the hour, in season. Reservations are required. Even young children, ages two and up, can go as long as they're accompanied by an adult.

Cape May Parasail

South Jersey Marina, Rt. 109, Cape May, NJ 08204
Telephone: 609-884-8759

SPAS

It's a vacation, right? So it should come as no surprise that this premiere vacation resort has two spas.

Cape May Spas

CAPE MAY DAY SPA
Two locations:
607 Jefferson St., Cape May, NJ 08204 • Telephone: 609-898-1003
Congress Hall Hotel
251 Beach Ave., Cape May, NJ 08204 • Telephone: 609-898-2425
Website: www.capemaydayspa.com

SERENITY DAY SPA AND SALON
3704 Bayshore Rd., North Cape May, NJ 08204
Telephone: 609-884-6900

WHALE- AND DOLPHIN-WATCHING CRUISES

The waters surrounding Cape May teem with marine life because of the meeting of two major bodies of water, the Atlantic Ocean and the Delaware Bay. Just as it's great for fishing for that reason, Cape May is also a good place for whale- and dolphin-watching. In fact, both competing whale-watching operations in town are so certain that you'll see some type of marine animal—dolphin, porpoise, or whale—that they guarantee it.

There are two boating lines that operate whale- and dolphin-watching cruises in Cape May. Both are located immediately upon entering Cape May over the large bridge from the Garden State Parkway. The Cape May Whale Watcher is first, a hard right the moment you come off the bridge. The Cape May Whale Watch and Research Center is almost immediately afterward, also on the right. Keep an eye open for signs the moment you come off the large bridge and you won't miss them. Many cruises end with the advent of cold weather, usually mid-October, although a few continue into December. They don't resume until the thermometer begins climbing again, usually mid-March or early April.

These cruises are very popular and tend to fill up quickly, particularly on summer weekends. Plan ahead and contact the cruise line to find out its policies on reservations, cancellations, and how soon you'll have to be there before the cruise departs.

The 110-foot, red-and-white *Cape May Whale Watcher* advertises itself as the largest and fastest marine mammal sighting boat in New Jersey. It can hold 290 passengers, 150 under cover. It has a snack bar offering hot and cold beverages, pizza, and hot dogs. The boat sails from March through December.

Several themed cruises are offered. Around Cape Island History Circle Tour (described in detail in chapter 2) is a morning cruise with complimentary coffee and danish. It sails from late April to mid-October.

The afternoon Whale and Dolphin Watch cruise is offered from March to December. Sunset Dolphin Watch around Cape Island is a repeat of the Around Cape Island cruise, but at a later time to catch twilight and sunset over the Atlantic Ocean and Delaware Bay. Complimentary pizza and hot dogs are provided. It sails

Cape May Whale Watcher

2nd Ave. and Wilson Dr., Cape May, NJ 08204
Telephone: 609-884-5445 or 800-786-5445
Website: www.capemaywhalewatcher.com

Cape May Whale Watch and Research Center

1286 Wilson Dr., Cape May, NJ 08204
Telephone: 609-898-1122 or 888-531-0055
Website: www.capemaywhalewatch.com

from Memorial Day to Labor Day. The *Cape May Whale Watcher* also offers a dinner option for its sunset cruise. Reservations must be made by 4 P.M.

The Cape May Whale Watch and Research Center is a more scientific facility that studies the feeding, migration, and breeding habits of area species. The center advertises that it originated the phenomenon of whale- and dolphin-watching on the New Jersey coast and is the only research facility in the state allowing public participation on vessels at sea. Cruises are aboard the *M/V Whale Watcher*, a seventy-five-foot-long, thirty-foot-wide catamaran that holds a maximum of 140 passengers.

The center also offers a variety of themed cruises.

The morning Dolphin Watch Cruise provides a free continental breakfast. The Big One is an early-afternoon cruise. The Sunset Dolphin Watch is held in the early evening, offering the same viewing possibilities as the morning cruise and including complimentary pizza and hot dogs. The Whale and Dolphin Watch Weekend Special is a morning cruise sailing from mid-June through mid-September and offering a complimentary continental breakfast.

Special Events

MAC often has special activity packages that combine some activities held during special-events time periods for big savings. Visit the MAC website, www.capemaymac.org, to find out more.

SHERLOCK HOLMES WEEKENDS

"The game's afoot, Watson!" It's time to don the deerstalker cap, pick up a favorite pipe stuffed with tobacco from a Persian slipper, and get ready to once again foil the evildoers of the world with deductive reasoning and infallible logic.

There's no better place to find the famous detective and his cohort Dr. Watson actively at work than during Cape May's Sherlock Holmes weekends. Begun years ago as little more than a lark by perhaps fifty hard-core Holmes aficionados, the weekends have grown to include several hundred people participating in costume contests, a contest to find clues to solve a real mystery, play acting, house tours, and more. The Sherlock Holmes weekends are now one of the town's most popular special events. They are held twice a year, in March and November. The same originally written mystery play is used both times.

The Sherlock Holmes weekend starts with a must-be-seen-to-be-believed dessert buffet at Congress Hall on Friday evening. While you and the other guests nibble on the goodies, you watch a group of actors and actresses dressed in full Victorian garb performing the first act of the mystery, setting up the situation.

The audience for this all-important first act also is encouraged to come in costume. Some folks do, to awesome effect. Thus there are women with hoop skirts, bustles, and elaborate peacock feather hats, and men wearing bowler hats and sporting mustaches—some real, some not—sitting next to others dressed in jeans and sneakers. The costumes can range from very elaborate to very common, such as a chimney sweep or bootblack. Part of the fun of the evening is admiring some of the audience's costumes and marveling at the ingenuity involved.

At the end of the first act of the play, after the characters have been established and the mystery set into motion, Holmes appears and sends all the guests on their way with clue sheets for solving the case.

Saturday is given over to a walking tour of numerous inns, where clues are hidden in plain sight. People fill out their clue sheets and hand them in. This is the most delightful day of the event, as people in full Victorian costume wander around the Historic District, searching for the participating inns where clues are hidden to help solve the mystery. (These inns are marked with large banners.) Holmes and Watson, dressed in full costume, walk around the streets and mingle with the amateur sleuths as they investigate each inn, but of course, they are coy about revealing

Cape May's Sherlock Holmes Weekends have become one of the town's most popular special events. MID-ATLANTIC CENTER FOR THE ARTS

any information. It's all done with the utmost respect for the situation, and people who don't address the sleuth as "Mr. Holmes" are certain to get an icy stare from their fellows, dressed or not. Everyone stays in character.

The innkeepers play along. Hidden somewhere in their house in plain sight is a clue to solving the mystery. But what is it? It could be a picture, an item on a table, something on a shelf . . . The innkeepers don't say, leaving it to the amateur detectives to write down what they think—right or wrong.

Late Saturday afternoon, the scene then shifts to a local theater, which is made up to resemble Holmes's study. Act Two of the play takes place here, but first the guests hand in their clue sheets.

Holmes and Watson then calmly and methodically present the second act of the drama. They go over all the evidence, shooting down the many red herrings that were at the various inns as the guests find out how close they came to solving the mystery. Did they have the right clues or not? There's plenty of moaning and groaning among the audience as the amateur detectives realize they've been had by something that was not really evidence.

On Sunday morning, in the final act of the drama, Holmes reveals the solution to the crime during a delicious brunch at a local eatery.

What adds an extra element of fun to all this is the contest among the folks who dressed up in Victorian costumes. Watching people walk around the Historic District in period clothes is one thing. Watching them battle for first prize in the best costume contest is something else entirely. Some folks spare no expense to make their costume the most colorful and elaborate, not to mention authentic.

In the past, special packages have been offered that include accommodations, breakfast, a dinner coupon, and admission to all Holmes activities. Check the MAC website at the beginning of this chapter for details.

Writer John Pekich authors the original mysteries that the weekends are based on. A writer, lecturer, and teacher of mystery workshops, he initially got involved with the Sherlock Holmes weekends by playing the killer in one of the earliest mysteries. He then acted in the dramas for several years. When the previous playwright left, Pekich stepped in and began writing the shows. He continually reads and rereads the Sir Arthur Conan Doyle Sherlock Holmes stories and uses his strong background to help him draft a mystery that is both faithful to Cape May and true to the Holmes character. It takes him about three months to write the three-act play, which is used for both the March and November weekends. He does extensive research on Cape May and world events before committing pen to paper. All the events and most of the characters in the play are real. MAC wants to educate as well as entertain the public, so the Cape May characters in particular are drawn very finely.

As for the raging question that brings Holmes fans to blows, Pekich prefers the Jeremy Britt portrayal of Holmes over Basil Rathbone's performance. "Britt has that edgy quality with the nervous energy that Holmes has," he says.

Pekich also directs the play and reports that the actors involved love performing in it. Although they usually have no Holmes background, he provides each of them with extensive biographies. "People like that sense of being with the living Mr. Holmes," he says. "They get to go back into the nineteenth century for just a few moments, and they love it."

CAPE MAY FOOD AND WINE FESTIVAL

Cape May, already dubbed "the restaurant capital of the Jersey Shore," took that idea and ran with it to create its extremely popular Food and Wine Festival. The festival is more than just a bunch of people tasting wines and eating cheese snacks. The festival runs for a full week, usually in September a week or two after Labor Day, and features many of the fine restaurants in town battling it out in slightly off-kilter fashion. Where else can you see teams from restaurants racing against the clock and each other in a relay of restaurant games? Events include setting the fastest table, folding the fanciest napkin, and racing through an obstacle course to deliver a cocktail without spilling a drop.

The festival also includes the Harvest Country Fair, featuring antiques, collectibles, music, food, hayrides, and activities for the kids, and the Beer Tasting Dinner, a five-course dinner at a fine restaurant in which each course is paired with a different style beer.

The Food and Wine Festival is an exceptionally popular event in Cape May. Held after the hustle and bustle of the summer, the event is a chance for the town to settle into a more relaxed atmosphere and celebrate one of its chief attractions—fine food.

The festival is usually very well attended by people who both enjoy good food and like learning and swapping behind-the-scenes stories and tips about everything from how to make an excellent hollandaise sauce to cleaning stubborn grease stains. Indeed, that is part of the appeal of the event. Attendees not only get to listen to gourmet

The competition heats up—and guests eat up—at the Food and Wine Festival. MID-ATLANTIC CENTER FOR THE ARTS

The Food and Wine Festival takes Cape May's reputation for fine dining to a whole new level. MID-ATLANTIC CENTER FOR THE ARTS

chefs from their favorite restaurants share some of their secrets, but also ask about particularly vexing problems they've been dealing with in the kitchen.

The Chalfonte is noteworthy for many reasons, one being its sensational food. The hotel's fried chicken has gotten universally rave reviews and has been featured on Food TV. It's one specific reason why people return year after year. The rest of the food is just as exceptional, so it's a no-brainer that the Chalfonte is a popular participant in the Food and Wine Festival.

The festival afternoon at the Chalfonte begins in the hotel kitchen. No modernized twenty-first-century computerized marvel, the Chalfonte kitchen is how great kitchens ought to look—frying pans bigger than stop signs hanging from hooks, pans and pots sizzling and bubbling away—with a cornucopia of smells that would put a supermarket spice aisle to shame.

Participants gather around a table, and that's when the fun starts. The Chalfonte's two legendary African-American cooks, Dot and Lucille, hold court there in a style that's part Lucy, part Seinfeld, and all cooking savvy. They field questions, demonstrate some cooking and food preparation techniques, and throw around outrageous comic quips. Along the way, they impart some very real and useful information.

Those hoping for specific information as to how they produce some of their amazing dishes are due to be disappointed, however, as the cooks often add their ingredients by the pinch, dash, or handful. As the title of the Chalfonte cookbook states, with the legendary cook (and Dot and Lucille's mother) Miss Helen on the cover, *I Just Quit Stirrin' When the Tastin's Good.*

After the kitchen session, when you've managed to mess up such simple tasks as greasing a pan and putting flour on dough, it's off to the Chalfonte's dining room, where you are treated to a superb lunch that features—what else?—fried chicken. When you leave, you are given a small gift bag that includes the restaurant's cookbook, soap, postcards, and other Chalfonte memorabilia.

At the fabulous Washington Inn, you are treated to a superb gourmet lunch complete with a dessert that's too wonderful for words. During the meal, various chefs come out and answer questions.

Of course, the headliner of the festival is the food. You can't go wrong choosing the Gourmet Lunch Event, in which you get to attend—and eat—gourmet lunches at several of Cape May's finest restaurants, and the Chef's Dine-Around, featuring a five-course gourmet feast, with each course served in one of Cape May's premier restaurants. Each night features a different theme and combination of restaurants. Wine is provided with each course, with a representative from the sponsoring winery on hand to explain the pairings. A trolley shuttle between restaurants is provided.

And that's pretty much how the Food and Wine Festival goes.

There isn't just a blanket ticket for the Food and Wine Festival that allows you to pick and choose whatever you want to attend. You need to buy tickets for individual events, although multiple-day tickets, some in combination with a specific lodging, can also be an option. Check the MAC website and call if you have questions before attending the event.

CHRISTMAS IN CAPE MAY

Few things in life equal the unbridled joy, good cheer, and peace of a Cape May Christmas. Few experiences can equal the shivery goosebumps that you feel when you walk through the Historic District on a cold night, your breath blowing smoke rings in the air, and see the bed-and-breakfasts all a-glitter with Christmas lights, twinkling like gingerbread house stars. Few moments in this impersonal world are as gratifying as walking along the street and encountering other people who honestly and sincerely wish you a Merry Christmas and a Happy New Year. Few incidents are as seasonally defining as suddenly and unexpectedly being serenaded by smiling Christmas carolers. Not many occasions in this hustle-and-bustle, mall-oriented world are as sincere as strolling along the Washington Street Mall and being urged by shopkeepers to come inside and sample some hot chocolate and cookies to take the chill out of your bones.

Few things in life are as special as a Cape May Christmas.

It starts with the Holiday Preview Weekend, a week or so before Thanksgiving, when the whole town dons its holiday finery in preparation for a joyous season. It continues through the Holiday Craft Show and into the Annual Christmas Candlelight House Tour, when nearly two dozen B&Bs, inns, hotels, and churches throw open their doors to all visitors to reveal their special and often stunning holiday decor inside. Then comes the West Cape May Christmas Parade, a wassail party at

One of the delights of a Cape May Christmas is seeing the houses decked out in holiday finery.
MID-ATLANTIC CENTER FOR THE ARTS

the Physick Estate, and Candlelight Hospitality Night, when the Cape May merchants offer food and beverages to holiday shoppers. There's also the tree-lighting ceremony and community caroling, a chocolate fantasy buffet, the Dickens Christmas Extravaganza, and much, much more.

And then there's the crowds. It's like summer, or even more so, but this time with coats. It's little kids in earmuffs running up to pet the horses as they trot past, bedecked in holiday finery. It's young people clasping gloved hands and laughing softly in the moonlight. It's elderly couples walking slowly along, admiring the houses' beautiful decor. It's men and women of all ages laughing and smiling as cares and worries fall away, and the wonder and majesty of this special season work their subtle magic.

It's Christmas in Cape May—and it's not to be missed. With all this packed into seven short weeks, it's little wonder that the town takes January off and goes into hibernation—the only time Cape May can truly be said to be quiet.

Following are descriptions of some of the special events that take place in Cape May during the holiday season. There are many more. Advance reservations for most of these events are highly recommended.

Holiday Preview Weekend

Discover Cape May decked out in its holiday finery as it kicks off the holiday season during this special weekend. Special events include an evening wassail tour and a Physick Family Christmas at the Physick Estate.

Holiday Craft Show

Crafters and artisans from the mid-Atlantic region gather at Convention Hall on the promenade Friday and Saturday. If you can't find a unique or unusual gift here, you never will.

Annual Christmas Candlelight House Tours

This event has been listed as one of the top-ten holiday events in all of North America. That's pretty darn impressive. More than twenty establishments, including bed-and-breakfasts, guesthouses, hotels, and churches, are open to visitors, who set their own pace as they wander from place to place. The heated MAC trolley will pick you up and transport you to places too far to walk to.

Each place on the tour is decorated for Christmas inside and out. Many have thousands of twinkling lights framing their structures. A lot of houses that are not on the tour are decorated as well, providing a festive effect as you stroll along the streets. What makes this more than just another house tour—besides the decorations—is the atmosphere. Strolling groups of performers wander the streets singing Christmas carols. Two refreshment stations offer holiday punch, hot apple cider, and snacks. The innkeepers are on hand to greet visitors. They are smiling and friendly, and some dress up in elaborate Victorian holiday costumes. There is a tremendous feeling of warmth, fellowship, and friendliness that is absent from your crowded shopping mall holiday experience. Fellow visitors greet each other on the street. Laughter and smiles are the order of the night. If this was not the way Christmas was celebrated back in Victorian times, it should have been.

Christmas Community Wassail Party

The wassail party is an evening of old-fashioned holiday merrymaking at the Emlen Physick Estate for a good cause. In the true spirit of the holiday season, participants are asked to bring a nonperishable foodstuff donation for the Community Food Bank of Cape May.

Candlelight Hospitality Night

One of the most delightful events is Candlelight Hospitality Night. On a Friday night early in December, participating store owners offer hot and cold drinks, cheese, crackers, and cookies to shoppers as they wander along the pedestrian mall and other shopping areas. If the weather cooperates, many merchants set up tables outside with the food on it. Otherwise, it's inside the store.

The food and drink make shoppers stop for a moment, and the merchants often engage them in casual conversation. It's all so low-key and friendly that it's rather remarkable in this day and age of harried sales clerks and crowded stores.

The bonus for shoppers, besides the food and pleasant conversation, is that you actually get to look casually around the store—really look—and see what it carries. As you've already established a relationship with the shopkeeper, you don't feel funny or awkward asking questions. The entire evening is pleasant, warm, and satisfying. No matter how cold the weather, the event gives you an inner glow that is not soon wiped away. When you add in the fact that the entire pedestrian mall is decorated with Christmas greenery and most

The Washington Inn's Chocolate Fantasy Buffet is heaven for chocolate lovers. MID-ATLANTIC CENTER FOR THE ARTS

of the stores are festooned with twinkling lights, it's hard to think of a better way to get into the holiday spirit. If Santa Claus weren't so busy this time of year making toys, I'm sure he'd attend Hospitality Night.

The Ghosts of Christmas

There's something about Christmas that screams "spirits," and it's not your uncle who gets drunk at your house every holiday season. Rather, it's because of Dickens and his famous tale of ghosts and redemption for Ebenezer Scrooge.

But how did this all get started? Did Victorians really believe in ghosts and spirits? Was there a Victorian Christmas tradition of supernatural activity? Who else were some of the famous Victorian writers of ghost stories? All these questions and many more are answered by the Cape May "Ghostwriter," psychic medium Craig McManus, in a delightful presentation called the Ghosts of Christmas.

The event takes place at the Mad Batter restaurant on historic–and supposedly haunted–Jackson Street. While you eat an authentic Victorian-style dinner, McManus gives a wide-ranging talk on how the Victorians viewed ghosts and the supernatural. No discussion of Christmas ghosts would be complete without mentioning Charles Dickens, and McManus talks about the celebrated author and his classic story *A Christmas Carol* in great detail. Covered as well are other Victorian-era writers of supernatural tales, some still known today, others completely forgotten.

The entire talk is informative, funny, a bit creepy, and interesting, as McManus relates some of the Victorian attitudes toward spirits and tells of the writers who capitalized on them. The excellent Mad Batter food just adds to an already exceptional evening.

Every Christmas Story Ever Told (and Then Some)

This Cape May Stage event has been repeated for several years during Cape May's holiday season and is only increasing in popularity. It features, among many other things, flying reindeer and grumpy elves.

Dickens Christmas Extravaganza

This is one of the most popular of all Cape May holiday traditions, a three-day event with lectures, tours, and performances from the Dickens era. Each year a different Dickens book is spotlighted and featured in the event. As if all this weren't enough, it also includes a scrumptious feast at the elegant Washington Inn. As Oliver Twist said, "Please sir, I want some more."

A Physick Family Christmas

It's practically worth the price of admission to see the Physick Estate all decked out for the holidays. There is more greenery and red ribbon here than there is in a small city. Inside and out, from the bottom floor to the top, the entire house is so beautifully decorated that it's hard to believe. Victorian decorating tricks, such as using cotton to simulate snow, are on display.

But the fun is just beginning. All the "members" of the Physick family are dressed in their holiday best and are happy to spend time with you discussing the house decorations, Victorian Christmas customs, or anything else you want to talk about. The house, normally cozy anyway, is transformed by the use of greenery and a few small Victorian-style Christmas trees into a place of intimacy and warmth in which you feel genuinely a part of the Physick family. If you've ever wanted to spend one night traveling back in time and reliving a Victorian Christmas celebration, this is the event for you. As an added bonus, the ticket price includes admission to the current exhibit in the Carriage House.

VICTORIAN WEEK

If ever an event epitomized the essence of Cape May, it's Victorian Week, one of the town's biggest off-season events. Actually, "week" is a misnomer, as the event is a ten-day celebration of the town and its unique status and heritage. The event continues to grow in popularity and has been named one of the top 100 events in America. As more and more people discover Cape May and learn about the Victorian Week, there's been increasing demand for activities.

Folks participate in Victorian costume for some of the activities, such as Vintage Dance Weekend. This is when Victorian Week is at its finest. The sight of dozens of people dressed in period Victorian clothes wandering about the streets of the town personifies what Cape May is all about. It's not just a place to go, but a way of life. The careful attention to detail that each person lavishes on his or her costume illustrates that. Just observing the passersby for a day is reward enough.

But there's more to do, of course—much more. The event celebrates everything and anything Victorian. Some of the highlights include historic house tours, lectures, mystery dinners, vintage fashion shows, and brass band concerts. Below is a sampling of some typical Victorian Week activities. New ones are added yearly, while some others are retired, so it is absolutely imperative to check the MAC website or call before making plans. Although it's possible to go down for a day, advance reservations for accommodations and activities are strongly recommended.

Around Cape Island Boat Tour

A boat takes you on a tour of Cape May presented from a historical and legendary perspective.

Dances of the nineteenth century are revived during Victorian Week. MID-ATLANTIC CENTER FOR THE ARTS

Visitors and residents get into the spirit of Victorian Week. MID-ATLANTIC CENTER FOR THE ARTS

Vintage Dance Weekend

Folks dressed in period costume engage in ballroom dances of the period.

Stairway to the Stars

Here is an event as unique and enjoyable as those times you used to sit outside on a clear summer night and look up at the sky full of twinkling stars. When you're standing at the very top of the Cape May Lighthouse, looking up at the blackness of space with all those twinkling stars, it brings home the vastness of the universe.

Of course, climbing a lighthouse at night is an experience unto itself. There are lights inside, so no one has to worry about missing a step in the dark, but the shadows and dark corners give it an eerie feel. When the guide talks about the history of the lighthouse, sometimes questions about hauntings and spirits drown out most other topics.

But the real payoff is reaching the top and looking around. If there's moonlight, it plays like a slivery slice on top of the nearby ocean. If the night is totally dark, the sound of the water and its waves coming ashore seem to be heard more clearly. This experience will get you pondering the infinite mysteries of the universe.

Champagne and Gourmet Brunch Walk

This walking tour of the Historic District is followed by either a southern-style breakfast buffet at the Chalfonte Hotel (Sundays) or a gourmet brunch at the sensational Mad Batter restaurant.

Chocolate Fantasy Buffet

This buffet is composed totally of the Washington Inn's incredible delectable chocolate desserts. This is when chocolate lovers know that they've gone to heaven without the inconvenience of dying first.

Cape May–Style House Tour

This is similar to the walking tour of the Historic District, but it gets you into some personal residences that are normally off-limits to the public. Once inside, you get to ask questions and observe the owner's decorating tastes and concepts.

WORLD SERIES OF BIRDING

Cape May is one of the best birding spots on the entire East Coast. The area's location on the Atlantic Flyway means that an incredible variety of birds visit the area, particularly during spring and autumn migration periods.

The World Series of Birding is usually held on the second or third Saturday in May, rain or shine. Teams and individuals from around the globe have twenty-four hours to identify by sight or sound as many species of birds as they can in the state of New Jersey, so naturally many come to Cape May. About 250 species have been seen in an average year since the event started in 1984. There are four different levels, ranging from kids to senior citizens, with awards given for top honors in various categories. The event enables birders to use, sharpen, and display their birding skills and focuses attention on the habitat needs of migrating birds.

The WSB raises hundreds of thousands of dollars for environmental causes. Birders obtain pledges for the number of species they observe. Teams have raised from as little as $500 to as much as $150,000. More than $8 million has been raised since the WSB's inception in 1984.

This event is hosted by the New Jersey Audubon Society. Go to www.nj audubon.com to find out more.

Cape May is one of the most important bird migration hot spots in the world. MID-ATLANTIC CENTER FOR THE ARTS

SPRING FESTIVAL

Spring is one of the most glorious times of the year in this coastal community. Everything seems fresh and new. The sea breezes coming off the water carry the hint and promise of summer and all it has to offer. The sun, warm on your face, foretells even hotter days to come. But first, like a caterpillar coming out of its cocoon, Cape May wakes up and revels in its rebirth.

And a glorious rebirth it is. All through the Historic District, owners are sprucing up their properties and repairing winter's damage. Homes gleam with fresh coats of paint, and the sounds of saws and hammers are heard up and down the streets.

But the real rebirth comes in the yards, where bulbs that were meticulously planted in autumn's anticipation of spring now burst forth, their shiny green shoots a welcome sight after the drab winter. Crocuses poke their heads from the ground, a riot of colors in yellow, purple, and white. Yellow and white daffodils stand straight and tall, and tulips begin the long process of emerging to dazzle for such a frustratingly short time.

People are in their gardens or yards, some digging and planting, some raking and bagging, but all are involved in the same activity—making their properties beautiful. Yards are ablaze with color, trees stand tall with damaged limbs removed, and bushes are neat and pruned. In the air is the smell of freshly cut grass.

The town comes alive as well. Restaurants and lodgings closed for several months spring to life with a bustle of activity. Bicycles suddenly appear on the streets, and pedestrians stroll along the Promenade. Benches are filled with folks reading, talking, or just looking. Flowers bloom on the pedestrian mall, traffic intersections come alive with greenery, and the horses resume pulling their carriages.

To capitalize on the beauty of the town, Cape May holds its Spring Festival. It's almost like a rerun of the town's famed Victorian Week, except that it takes place in the spring, when Cape May is exploding in color—and when the tulips are all in bloom here, there's no prettier sight in the world.

The Spring Festival features ten days of Victorian activities that include a nineteenth-century dance weekend with workshops and a costume ball, a tulip and garden craft show, a brass band concert, murder mystery dinners, and glassblowing demonstrations on the lawn of the Emlen Physick Estate. Tours are also offered, including a Grand Restoration House Tour, Secret Garden Tours, and Garden Trolley Rides.

Spotlighted Bed-and-Breakfasts

Cape May is the bed-and-breakfast capital of the East Coast, and perhaps of the entire planet. This chapter highlights twelve inns out of the sixty or so the town offers, giving a feel for the innkeepers and the types of houses they run. Following is some general information that you should keep in mind about the inns. If you have specific questions, it's always best to call the inn or visit its website.

Many inns and other lodgings require a two-night minimum stay on weekends and holidays. It may be challenging to find a room for a one-night stay, depending on the time of year. The rate you pay also depends on the time of year, exact day, and type of room. It can vary enormously because of these factors. Many inns offer special packages, especially on weekdays and in the off-season.

Innkeepers usually will not accept personal checks for payment. If you make a reservation in advance, some may let you pay with a personal check if there is enough time for it to clear. If they know you from previous visits, they may be more willing to accept a check. Always call and ask in advance.

Few inns accommodate children under age ten or twelve, and most do not allow pets. A couple of pet-friendly inns are listed at the end of this chapter.

It is virtually impossible to find an inn that is handicapped-compliant. This is because the homes are historic, and the work that would have to be done to bring them into compliance with federal and state guidelines would destroy their historic character. Innkeepers may refer to certain rooms as "accessible but not compliant," which means that a wheelchair can fit through the door and the room is usable by a

Lodging Services

Since Cape May gets so many visitors, it has set up numerous special services that can assist you in your quest for a room.

CAPE MAY RESERVATION SERVICE
Telephone: 800-729-7778

HISTORIC ACCOMMODATIONS OF CAPE MAY
P.O. Box 83, Cape May, NJ 08204
Telephone: 609-884-0080 • Website: www.capemaylodging.com

GREATER CAPE MAY CHAMBER OF COMMERCE
P.O. Box 556, Cape May, NJ 08204
Telephone: 609-884-5508 • Website: www.capemaychamber.com

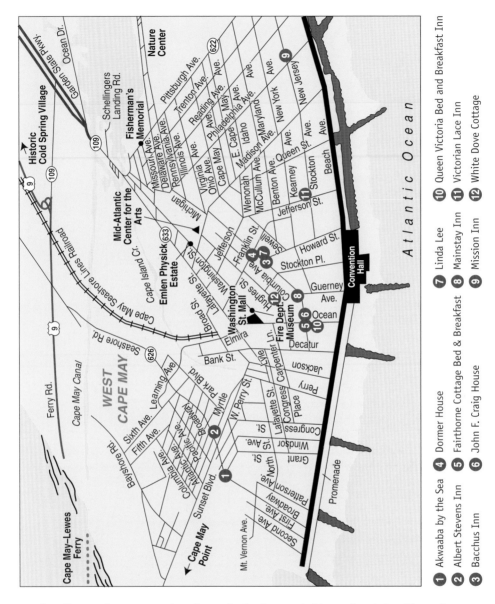

handicapped person, and perhaps the bathroom is bigger, but it is still not in compliance. It is best to call ahead with any access questions.

It is currently illegal to smoke in New Jersey's bed-and-breakfasts or other lodgings. Besides, even if you could smoke here, these homes are old and historic, and they are exquisitely furnished. One careless cigarette could start a huge conflagration among this old wood and material.

Some inns offer off-street parking, and that's a real bonus. But if you have to use on-street parking, find a spot and leave your car. If you move it, the spot likely will not be there when you return. So find it and forget it. Cape May is best seen by walking or bicycle anyway.

AKWAABA BY THE SEA

Monique Greenwood was sitting on the beach at Cape May on her birthday when she decided to change her life—and Cape May B&B fans couldn't be happier. At that time, she was juggling several responsibilities, including being editor-in-chief of a magazine. She was already running a B&B in Brooklyn when she decided to chuck everything else and concentrate on that. Before she could say "Queen Victoria," she found herself the owner of this stylish building on Broadway. She had found her new calling.

The result is Akwaaba by the Sea, Cape May and the Jersey Shore's only African-American–themed bed-and-breakfast. Akwaaba, which means "welcome" in a language of Ghana, West Africa, is one of several inns owned by Monique and her husband, Glenn Pogue, who welcome all to share in their generous hospitality. The others are located in Brooklyn and Washington, D.C.

The house, built in 1850, has been decorated in a style unique to Cape May that combines Victoriana with Africana. Its distinctive pale green outside coloring and pretty front yard instantly identify it as a place of distinction. "It is a celebration of the rich African-American heritage that is in this county," Greenwood says.

From the designs on the dining-room chairs to the unique black wire figurines displayed on the wall, Akwaaba tells the story of the rich African culture.

The inn's five rooms are named after African-American local heroes. Three are single rooms, and the other two are guest suites. Each room has a private bath, air-conditioning, and a CD player. One of the suites has a fully equipped

African-American–themed Akwaaba by the Sea Bed & Breakfast is unique. AKWAABA BY THE SEA

Visiting Akwaaba by the Sea

116 Broadway, West Cape May, NJ 08204
Telephone: 866-INN-DULJ • In NYC: 718-455-5958
Website: www.akwaaba.com • E-mail: info@awkaaba.com

Season: Mid-May through mid-October.
Rooms: 5 guest rooms.
Handicap access: No.
Parking: Limited on-site parking.
Credit cards: Visa and MasterCard.
Personal checks or money orders: Accepted only if received within seven days of arrival date.

Decorations in the suites at the Akwaaba by the Sea honor African-American heritage. AKWAABA BY THE SEA

kitchen; the other has a sitting room with microwave and minirefrigerator.

Akwaaba is known for its sumptuous full southern breakfast. More good news for families is that Akwaaba is delighted to accept children as guests. From the broad smiles of the girls and boys parading in and out of the inn, it's clear they're glad to be here as well.

"We want to leave our guests with special memories," says Monique, smiling. "I think that my calling is to help people live their richest life."

ALBERT STEVENS INN

It may seem like a long leap from the flash and glitter of Atlantic City to the more sedate atmosphere of Victorian Cape May, but Jim and Lenanne Labrusciano have made the transition with ease. The couple, both of whom formerly worked in Atlantic City casinos, bought the Albert Stevens Inn in March 2001. Since then, they've worked hard to transform the establishment into one of Cape May's premier bed-and-breakfast inns. And as Jim says, "We want our guests to feel that our home is their home."

Built in 1898, the house was commissioned by Dr. Albert G. Stevens, a Cape May homeopathic medical doctor, as a wedding gift for his bride, Bessie. Stevens, a local favorite, was the oldest practicing physician in Cape May. Pictures of the doctor and his family adorn the house. Several of the inn's rooms are named for members of the Stevens family.

Upon purchasing the home, the Labruscianos embarked on an ambitious renovation project that has so far seen them completely do over the kitchen, the owners' quarters, and two dining rooms. They are striving to faithfully re-create the Victorian era while avoiding the "museum look." The result is an elegant, airy, and tasteful Victorian jewel.

The Albert Stevens is a three-story Queen Anne classic, with a unique floating staircase—one that has no visible means of support—suspended from the third-floor turret. At the top of the staircase is the Tower Suite, which takes up the entire third floor. The inn is larger than many in Cape May. It is distinctively colored, with a yellow exterior and green shingles and trim. A large, wide front porch wraps around one side, and an attractive green fence with red tips surrounds the property.

Visiting the Albert Stevens Inn:

127 Myrtle Ave., Cape May, NJ 08204
Telephone: 609-884-4717 or 800-890-2287
Website: www.albertstevensinn.com
E-mail: albertstevensinn@hotmail.com

Season: March through end of December. Closed January and February.
Rooms: 7 guest rooms, 3 suites.
Handicap access: No.
Parking: On-site.
Credit cards: Visa and Mastercard.
Personal checks: Accepted.

Jim and Lenanne live on the premises. They are laid-back as far as innkeepers go, but they are always available to help their guests. "We're more like concierges," says Jim. "We want to create a positive experience. We don't have a lot of rules."

The inn's seven rooms and three suites all have private baths and are heated and air-conditioned. Each contains period antiques and lace window treatments as well as some combination of a TV, VCR, DVD, wireless Internet, and refrigerator.

The inn is located directly across the street from Wilbraham Park, the site for many summer craft shows and special events like the Strawberry Festival in June and the Lima Bean Festival in October. Guests often enjoy rocking on the front porch and watching the activity in the park.

Lenanne makes all of the inn's baked goods from scratch. The inn is renowned for its sherried eggs on English muffins and apple French toast. The Albert Stevens has two guest dining rooms plus a heated veranda that guests enjoy in chillier weather. The two dining rooms means that all guests can be seated at one time for meals, if so desired.

At Christmastime, the inn is spectacularly decorated. The large fir tree in the front yard blazes with electric color, and the spacious front porch is similarly decorated with seasonal cheer. A twisting, lifesize Santa figure on the porch chortles "Ho, ho, ho" periodically.

Jim and Lenanne enjoy their role as innkeepers because they like people. They say they can see people visibly relax and unwind once they get there, and they enjoy the part they play in helping their guests take a breather from the stressful world outside the Albert Stevens's comforting walls.

"People are good," says Jim.

The Albert Stevens Inn is a bed-and-breakfast restored to its Victorian splendor. ALBERT STEVENS INN

BACCHUS INN

The first time Lisa met John Matusiak—in Cape May, naturally—she gave him what is known in dating parlance as "the brush-off." "She blew me off. Absolutely blew me off," says John, laughing.

Little did John know then that a few years later he and Lisa would be married (John proposed on the beach) and owners of one of Cape May's most delightful bed-and-breakfast establishments: the Bacchus Inn.

John has innkeeping in his blood. He grew up in nearby Wildwood Crest, where his father ran a motel. After he and Lisa got married, they began talking about how much fun it would be to become innkeepers in Cape May. Before long, they were the proud owners of what is today the Bacchus Inn.

John used to be in the wine business, and the inn is named for the Roman god of wine. But Bacchus not only had a taste for the grape, he also represented wine's social and beneficial influences. So Bacchus was also viewed as the promoter of civilization, law, and peace.

The wine theme is carried throughout this charming six-room inn. Each of the guest rooms is named for a variety of wine. On display is a handmade grape press made by John's grandfather. And in the afternoon, the Bacchus serves wine and cheese.

As one of the youngest innkeeping couples in Cape May, if not *the* youngest, John and Lisa have also made sure that the Bacchus reflects their youthful playfulness and exuberance. The inviting pool table in a downstairs common area is a prime example. Few other B&Bs have such a feature. "At the Bacchus we get a lot of couples," Matusiak explains. "The women may go antiquing all day, while the guys shoot stick."

The six rooms at the Bacchus vary in size. Three of the rooms are standard-sized, and the other three range from the adorable Petite Sirah Room to the large Champagne Suite. Each room has a private bath, (at least) a queen-size bed, and central air-conditioning and heat. All are elegantly decorated with period antiques, and most have fireplaces.

Visiting the Bacchus Inn

710 Columbia Ave., Cape May, NJ 08204
Telephone: 609-884-2129 or 866-844-2129
Website: www.bacchusinn.com
E-mail: innkeeper@bacchusinn.com

Season: Open year-round.
Rooms: 6 guest rooms.
Handicap access: No.
Parking: On-street.
Credit cards: Not accepted.
Personal checks: Accepted for deposit only. Remaining balance must be paid by cash, money order, cashier's check, or traveler's check.

Guests can relax on the front porch at the Bacchus Inn. BACCHUS INN

It would be hard to find friendlier innkeepers than the Matusiaks. John is more outgoing, and Lisa is more reserved, so the couple has all the bases covered when it comes to guest interaction. If people want to talk, John is more than happy to oblige. If they want to hang back, stay to themselves, and ask occasional questions, Lisa is their main contact. "It's a nice blend," John says.

Lisa is hardly reserved when it comes to the kitchen, however. Her banana-stuffed French toast with almond-streusel topping is a real crowd pleaser at the Bacchus, followed hard by her strawberry soup. And her chocolate chip cookies are so good that you want to eat every last crumb.

Architecturally, the Bacchus is classified as Folk Victorian because it blends several different Victorian styles. One of its most impressive features is an original large,

Top left: A community pool table is one of the more popular features at the Bacchus Inn. *Bottom left:* Each room at the Bacchus takes its name from a variety of wine. Pictured is the Zinfandel Room. BACCHUS INN

three-sided stained-glass bay window. It's rare to have a window of this size or one constructed of stained glass in a Victorian home. From it, you can gaze down on historic Columbia Avenue and watch the horse-drawn carriages and people passing by.

Another guest favorite at the inn is its side porch, perfect for reading a book or just relaxing. Often guests carry a glass of wine and a book outside, settle into a rocker, and pass the next few hours in unhurried bliss.

A lasting testimony to the warm, comfortable atmosphere that John and Lisa have created at the Bacchus is their guest comments book, in which one word shows up over and over, a word that perfectly sums up what the Bacchus is all about: "relaxing."

Up on Mount Olympus, the gods must be smiling.

DORMER HOUSE

Dennis and Lucille Doherty had been regularly coming to Cape May on vacation when they decided that they might like to rent a house for a time. So they went to a local real estate agent to inquire about renting a place. Little did they know that this decision would change their lives.

While at the real estate office, Dennis happened to notice a photo of a bed-and-breakfast for sale. Intending to just casually inquire about it, he and Lucille became interested in buying it and wound up going to see it. Although that one proved unsatisfactory, Dennis asked the real estate agent to keep them in mind if another became available.

Within a few months, something else did—the Dormer House. But it was not the beautiful bed-and-breakfast inn that it is now. When the couple bought it, the building was a guest house with apartments. Dennis and Lucille rolled up their sleeves and got to work. Four and a half long years later, they completed the conversion of the property from an ordinary building into the stylish, gorgeous

Visiting the Dormer House

800 Columbia Ave., Cape May, NJ 08204
Telephone: 609-884-7446 or 800-884-5052
Website: www.dormerhouse.com
E-mail: dormerhouse@snip.net

Season: Daily from mid-March through January 1 and weekend of Valentine's Day.
Rooms: 14 guest rooms.
Handicap access: No.
Parking: On-site.
Credit cards: All major credit cards accepted.
Personal checks: Accepted.

Dormer House you see today. "Amazing," Dennis says with a laugh, shaking his head at the memory.

The Dormer House is a Colonial Revival home, and it's a good example of the style that became quite popular after the 1876 Centennial Exposition. It was built in 1899 for the family of rich marble dealer John Jacoby of Philadelphia—the founder and first commodore of the Cape May Yacht Club—as an elegant summer house for entertaining.

With its distinctive red-and-white color theme and spacious grounds, the Dormer House is quite easy to find on historic Columbia Avenue, especially since it occupies a large corner lot. Few other Victorian structures have as much land as Dormer House, which is particularly nice for the guest who enjoys wandering about the grounds.

The Dormer House decked out in holiday decorations. PAT KING-ROBERTS

As a Colonial Revival home, Dormer House is quite a departure from many other bed-and-breakfast inns in Cape May. It is bigger, brighter, and airier than a typical inn. Its common areas are larger, and its spacious enclosed side porch can easily seat all of its guests for breakfast without the danger of a human traffic jam. Of particular interest is its center hall feature, a large greeting area that is uncommon for a Victorian bed-and-breakfast. It is perfect, however, for greeting weary guests and providing them a place to put down their luggage without being afraid of hitting something.

The thirteen guest rooms at the Dormer House follow the lead of the rest of the inn—they're large and airy. Each has a television, queen bed, and private bathroom, some with whirlpool tubs. All are decorated in pastel colors with eclectic furnishings and an assortment of antique mirrors and period furniture. Inn amenities include on-site parking, beach chairs, and beach towels. The parking lot is particularly large, and on crowded Columbia Avenue, it's a welcome blessing.

Dennis and Lucille are gracious, engaging innkeepers. They are always available for their guests, whether it's for casual small talk or a serious discussion of restaurants in Cape May. But they also allow guests their privacy. As Dennis says, "There's a time to talk to guests and a time to leave them alone."

Christmas at the Dormer House is something to behold. Not content with simply decorating the building with thousands of white lights, Dennis and Lucille dress up in period costume, complete with his walking stick that doubles as a tiny flask—for those really cold nights. The entire house is lavishly decorated, and the living room boasts a fifteen-foot Christmas tree that goes through the floorboards from the first floor to the second.

The Dormer House has an easy, laid-back aura. "Our guests like coming here because we don't impose a lot of rules on them," says Dennis. "We maintain a very relaxed atmosphere, and it has worked out very well." Perhaps the Dohertys' unique sense of what pleases and delights a guest also has something to do with it. For instance, a perfectly normal-looking armoire in a perfectly normal-looking room contains—of all things—a bathtub. People who go to hang their clothes inside the armoire get quite a surprise. But that's the way the Dormer House is—big, bright, friendly, and filled with unexpected treasures.

FAIRTHORNE COTTAGE BED & BREAKFAST

The overwhelming feeling that surrounds the Fairthorne Inn is one of friendliness. This beautiful Colonial Revival–style inn, just a block and a half from both the beach and downtown Cape May, exudes a casual warmth, and it all flows from the graceful innkeeping style of owners Diane and Ed Hutchinson.

Built in 1892 by a whaling captain, the Fairthorne features leaded stained-glass windows and a graceful wraparound veranda appointed with wicker. The inn's companion, the Fairthorne Cottage, is a Carpenter's Gothic building that was originally located on another street and moved to its current site. There are nine guest rooms between the two buildings.

The Colonial Revival–style Fairthorne Inn boasts a central location near the shops and beaches.
PAT KING-ROBERTS

The Hutchinsons have been innkeepers at the Fairthorne for nearly fifteen years. Before that, the two both worked for Bell Atlantic. Diane always had roots in the area. She grew up in Stone Harbor, just up the Parkway, in a guest house in which her grandmother rented rooms for $2 per night. Because the Hutchinsons have seven children, they are used to having a lot of company in their home. So becoming B&B owners was a logical step.

"We've always had company," Diane says with a chuckle, "but now people pay us. It's much nicer."

Visiting the Fairthorne Cottage Bed & Breakfast

111 Ocean St. (mailing address: P.O. Box 2381), Cape May, NJ 08204
Telephone: 609-884-8791 or 800-438-8742
Website: www.fairthorne.com

Season: Open year-round.
Rooms: 9 guest rooms.
Handicap access: No.
Parking: On- and off-site.
Credit cards: Visa, MasterCard, American Express, and Discover.
Personal checks: Accepted.
Other: Member of Select Registry.

The Fairthorne is in an ideal location. It's on Ocean Street, only about a block from the shopping areas and directly across from the Cape May Public Library. To the other side, the ocean beckons. The big, brown-shingled building with the wide front porch is a commanding presence on the street.

The Fairthorne Inn is known far and wide for its hospitality. It's filled with the Hutchinsons' presence, and that's a good thing. They do everything themselves, including cooking, bookkeeping, and answering the telephone. Their cat, Ally, is a friendly little ball of fur that is the hit of the inn. The common areas inside the inn are filled with antiques, fresh flowers, and lace window treatments. Diane and Ed are available whenever their guests need them but are respective of their privacy at the same time. "We're here for them without being intrusive," says Diane.

Each of the inn's six rooms, decorated in the Fairthorne's warm, comfortable style, has a private bath, king or queen-size bed, television, refrigerator, and air-conditioning. Some also contain fireplaces or whirlpool tubs.

It fits perfectly with the Hutchinsons' easygoing, friendly style that all three of Fairthorne Cottage's rooms are named for their grandchildren: Ashley, Julia, and Gabrielle. These are the Fairthorne's premium rooms, with gas fireplaces and Victorian dressers, as well as private baths, televisions, refrigerators, and air-conditioning. On-site parking is included for cottage guests.

Besides warm, friendly hospitality, the Fairthorne is known throughout Cape May for its chocolate chip cookies. What could be more friendly, more homelike, than a glass of cold milk and warm chocolate cookies? That feeling is why Fairthorne guests continue to return year after year.

"All our guests say coming here is like coming home," says Ed. "They feel so comfortable and relaxed here. It's a very warm, comfortable house, and they feel comfortable with us. We've made a lot of good friends."

"We like people. We truly love our guests," Diane says with a smile.

JOHN F. CRAIG HOUSE

"I hope our guests feel like they're coming to Barbara and Chip's house." Barbara Masemore laughed as she said that, but it's no joke: The John F. Craig House is indeed Barb and Chip's house. And the spirit of funky fun, irreverence, and hospitality that the Masemores provide at this beautiful inn makes that a very good thing indeed.

Plainly, the couple has ripped a page or two out of the *How Not to Bore Your Guests* innkeeper's handbook. The John F. Craig House contains wildly eclectic collections of objects designed to interest, amuse, and entertain their guests—everything from bawdy ladies to prewar Lionel trains to toys. If you can't find something to pique your interest at the John F. Craig House, then you simply aren't trying. "Whimsical and romantic," Barbara calls it, and she's right on the money.

The house was built in 1850, making it one of the oldest houses on historic Columbia Avenue. A Carpenter Gothic Victorian expansion was added in 1866. The house was named in honor of John F. Craig, a wealthy Philadelphia sugar merchant and philanthropist.

The John F. Craig House is home to some eclectic collections. PAT KING-ROBERTS

The couple didn't start out to be innkeepers. But after they realized that they were spending all of their spare time in Cape May, innkeeping seemed the logical way to make a living and continue spending time there. In the Hall of Good Decisions, Barbara says that this one was a home run.

"I just love innkeeping," she says. "I enjoy people. I like the variety of people that come into my life. Each person gives me new energy."

Visiting the John F. Craig House

609 Columbia Ave., Cape May, NJ 08204
Telephone: 609-884-0100 or 877-544-0314
Website: www.johnfcraig.com
E-mail: chipbarbara@comcast.net

Season: Open year-round.
Rooms: 8 guest rooms.
Handicap access: No.
Parking: Off-site.
Credit cards: Visa, MasterCard, and Discover.
Personal checks: Accepted.

The John F. Craig House has six common rooms—an unusually large number in a bed-and-breakfast. But this exceptional amount of common space allows guests both privacy and familiarity. They can either choose to find their own little corner or else mingle socially with the Masemores and the other guests. "We never feel crowded," Barbara says. "It's always comfortable."

The inn has eight guest rooms—seven bedrooms and one suite—each with a private bath, cable TV with VCR, coffeemaker, refrigerator, hair dryer, iron, and individual air-conditioning and heat controls. Some have fireplaces. All the rooms are decorated in a light Victorian style with lace curtains, old-fashioned wallpaper, and antique furnishings. Amenities at the inn include beach towels, beach chairs, and bicycles. A box in the front yard in the shape of the house contains a brochure about the inn.

The John F. Craig House is not known for any one particular dish—*everything* is good. In fact, the inn was recently awarded the 2005 *Book of Lists* designation for Best Breakfast in the Northeast. The Masemores have published a cookbook—fittingly called *Cookbook*—with many of the recipes that have made the Craig House famous.

Good food, fun atmosphere, elegant and spacious surroundings—it's not hard to discover why guests return to the John T. Craig House year after year. "I hope I can give my guests peace, relaxation, and a smile," Barbara says.

LINDA LEE

"We're major Victorian nuts." With that in mind, Stephanie Kirk knew there was just one place for her and her husband, Archie, to wind up: Cape May, the Victorian capital of the East Coast. So in September 2004, the Kirks joined the ranks of Cape May's innkeepers as proprietors of the enchanting Linda Lee bed-and-breakfast inn.

The couple had a long love affair with Cape May prior to taking the innkeeper route, coming down to visit often and even owning a home in the town. They were also frequent participants in Victorian activities here, including Victorian Week, the Sherlock Holmes Weekend, and the Victorian Ball. "We started coming down here after we got married," says Archie. "We stayed at different B&Bs and really enjoyed it."

One thing led to another, and ultimately the Kirks found themselves the owners of the Linda Lee and decided to operate it as a bed-and-breakfast. When they opened, they were immediately booked and haven't looked back.

"We love the people," says Stephanie. "We like to see them have fun in Cape May."

Fun is exactly what visitors to the charming Linda Lee do enjoy. Built in the Victorian Carpenter's Gothic style on one of Cape May's most historic streets, the home has been elegantly furnished by the Kirks to provide every comfort for their guests.

Built in 1872, the house remained in one family for more than fifty years. It was named Linda Lee after a favorite granddaughter, who was quite a fixture on the Cape May social scene while single.

The Linda Lee has four guest rooms and one suite. Each has a private bath, king- or queen-size bed, flat-screen television, and air-conditioning. Some have private verandas and gas fireplaces. All have been beautifully decorated. Inn amenities

---

Visiting the Linda Lee

725 Columbia Ave., Cape May, NJ 08204
Telephone: 609-884-1240
Website: www.thelindalee.com • E-mail: LindaLeeCapeMay@aol.com

Season: Open year-round.
Rooms: 5 guest rooms.
Handicap access: No.
Parking: On-site and off-site.
Credit cards: Visa and MasterCard.
Personal checks: Accepted.

---

include a large front veranda for rocking or snoozing, beach towels and sand chairs, on-site parking, and bicycles.

Guests frequently request the Linda Lee's Tulip Eggs for breakfast, a house specialty that makes you realize the people who just eat eggs scrambled or fried are missing the boat. Another delicious dish is the raspberry French toast.

The overall elegance and comfortable charm of the Linda Lee is enhanced by Archie and Stephanie Kirk, two genuinely nice and instantly likable people, who have infused the inn with a comfortable, hospitable feeling. Not surprisingly, the house is a fixture on numerous Cape May tours and special events, including the Sherlock Holmes Weekends and Candlelight Christmas Tours. Whether guests are admiring the home's functional antiques, such as the working player piano in the parlor, rocking on the veranda and watching the tourists go by, or just passing through as part of a tour, they feel like welcome friends.

"When people leave here, they say, 'We feel like we've known you for twenty-five years,'" says Archie. "That's the way we try to make everyone feel."

MAINSTAY INN

The fabulous Mainstay Inn has unusual history: It started out as an all-male gambling club. Today this legacy is remembered in the inn's unique, museum-quality interior, especially in the large common areas.

The Mainstay actually consists of three buildings: the original inn, a refurbished cottage, and a World War I–era building across the street known as the Officers' Quarters. The main inn, the former gambling club, is an Italianate villa with fourteen-foot-high ceilings, twelve-foot windows that are nearly floor-to-ceiling, all original chandeliers, and richly ornamented furniture that was custom-made for the gambling club. The inn has been lauded in magazines from coast to coast as a stunning example of Victorian architecture at its finest.

When it was operated as a gambling palace, the Mainstay was open only during the summer months. Once gambling was made illegal in New Jersey in 1898, it was converted to a summer cottage. It remained that way until 1949, when it became a guest house called the Victorian Mansion. In 1977, it was renovated into a bed-and-breakfast.

The Mainstay Inn, which began as a gambling club, is now a bed-and-breakfast. MAINSTAY INN

The Mainstay Inn has been restored and refurbished so accurately that it's not hard to imagine you're back in 1872 the moment you walk through the front door. "It was meant to impress you when you walk in," says longtime assistant innkeeper Kathy Miley, who runs the Mainstay along with assistant innkeeper Diane Clark.

Kathy sets the tone for the Mainstay—relaxed, casual, and friendly. The two innkeepers are always available to meet their guests' needs. "We're pretty darn flexible," Kathy says with a laugh.

The refined and exquisite Mainstay is also full of surprises. There's a cupola on the top of the house, where guests can climb to sit, read, or just gaze at the scenery. And when you retire for the evening, you don't just hang a Do Not Disturb sign on the door. Instead, you set a stuffed cat outside your room, giving new meaning to the phrase "putting the cat out."

Foodwise, the Mainstay never cashes in its chips. In the spring and fall, the inn features a full sit-down family-style breakfast around the enormous dining-room table. As befits the more relaxed pace of the summer months, a breakfast buffet is provided for indoor or veranda dining.

The well-appointed rooms at the Mainstay continue the inn's tradition of hospitality. MAINSTAY INN

Visiting the Mainstay Inn

635 Columbia Ave., Cape May, NJ 08204
Telephone: 609-884-8690
Website: www.mainstayinn.com • E-mail: mainstayinn@comcast.net

Season: Officers' Quarters, open year-round; Mainstay Inn, mid-March through
January; Cottage, April through November 15.
Rooms: 12.
Handicap access: One suite in Officer's Quarters.
Parking: Most rooms have designated parking spaces.
Credit cards: Visa, Mastercard, and American Express.
Personal checks: Checks are the preferred form of payment.
Other: Member of Select Registry.

The Mainstay's menus continue the tradition begun by one of the former owners, who was so well known for her fabulous breakfasts and unique culinary concoctions that she published a cookbook still sold at the inn. *Breakfast at Nine, Tea at Four* contains more than 150 recipes that have made the Mainstay famous among America's B&Bs.

The inn's six rooms are all incredibly detailed and lavishly appointed with museum-quality furnishings. Each is unique in its own way, such as the Henry Sawyer Room, with its matching marble-top dressers, or the Stonewall Jackson Suite, with a grand total of nine windows. All rooms have private baths, televisions, and other amenities. One room is named for Cardinal Gibbons, the first American cardinal, who used the mansion as a Catholic retreat for several summers.

Rooms in the Cottage and the Officers' Quarters are no less spectacular. A suite in the Officers' Quarters offers eight hundred square feet of living space, a whirlpool tub, fireplace, private porch, and other amenities.

"The grandeur of the spaces is what makes this such a unique building," Kathy says. She's certainly correct. A visit to the Mainstay is truly a once-in-a-lifetime experience and gives guests a rare glimpse into Cape May's fascinating past. It's never a gamble to stay at the Mainstay.

Breakfast is the most important—and popular—meal of the day at the Mainstay. MAINSTAY INN

MISSION INN

Most bed-and-breakfasts in Cape May are built in the Victorian architectural style, but the Mission Inn is as far from a standard Victorian structure as El Paso is from London.

Welcome to the simply awe-inspiring, southwestern-style Mission Inn, a bed-and-breakfast unlike any other in town. The building looks like a Spanish mission that would be found in the deserts of Southern California or New Mexico. With its distinctive weathered-looking adobe walls, bright red roof, and desert-style gardens, it could very easily be an inn found along a highway in the Southwest.

Inside, the building is light, airy, and large. The most striking thing about the interior is not just the mammoth size of all the rooms, but the openness. No sharp turns, dim lighting, and fussy corners in here. Each room, be it a guest bedroom or a common area, screams of space.

Prior to its reincarnation as a bed-and-breakfast, the building was simply a summer bungalow. It was built in 1912 by famed architect Nelson Z. Graves after a turn-of-the-century trip to the Pacific Coast. At one time, movie stars including Tyrone Power, Diana Barrymore, and Errol Flynn lived here.

Susan and Raymond Babineau-Roberts bought the property in June 2002 after scouring the East Coast for just the right inn. "We looked from Maine to Florida," says Susan. They didn't necessarily have a southwestern mission theme in mind, but after purchasing what would become the Mission Inn, the theme seemed obvious.

"I went out to California and photographed all twenty-one missions," says Susan. "I came back and started to re-create each room into a mission theme."

How well she has succeeded is evident by the eight stunning guest rooms. Each represents a particular mission in extraordinary detail. Many contain hand-carved headboards that depict the mission the room is named after so realistically you'll want to check your GPS and make sure you didn't take a wrong turn somewhere and wind up in New Mexico instead of the Jersey Shore.

The San Juan Capistrano Room, for example, contains a beautiful floor-to-ceiling headboard painted to resemble the Capistrano Mission, and the famous swallows that return to Capistrano every March are painted on the walls. The Santa Barbara Room has a mural that evokes the fabulous California coastline dotted with sailboats skimming along. Even the hallway is painted in such a way that it resembles a weathered abode, with glittering tiles scattered throughout and a climbing rose bush. Little wonder

More southwestern than Victorian, the Mission Inn stands out among the architecture in Cape May. MISSION INN

Each of the rooms at the Mission Inn reflects a different Spanish mission of the Southwest United States. MISSION INN

that the Mission Inn has won numerous awards for interior design.

"My feeling is that we've re-created and completed Nelson's dream of what he started out to have," says Susan. "He thought that this type of architecture would take off and that others would want to build homes similar to this. That never happened."

All rooms have air-conditioning, heat, cable TV, private baths, king-size beds, and numerous other amenities.

If the incredible interior of the Mission Inn doesn't make you absolutely love this place, the hospitality will. Susan and Raymond refer to their innkeeping style as "California casual" and encourage guests to curl up on the comfortable furniture and treat it as their own. At the same time, they are attentive to their guests' needs. Susan finds out from each guest his or her dietary preferences and plans her menus accordingly. In pleasant weather, if guests prefer, they can dine outside under the inn's latticed pergola or in the glass-enclosed solarium, reclining in wrought-iron chairs and idling away the time in pleasant company.

"Come as strangers, leave as friends," Susan says with a smile.

Visiting the Mission Inn

1117 New Jersey Ave., Cape May, NJ 08204
Telephone: 609-884-8380 or 800-800-8380
Fax: 609-884-4191
Website: www.missioninn.net • E-mail: info@MissionInn.net

Season: Open year-round.
Rooms: 8 guest rooms.
Handicap access: No.
Parking: On-site.
Credit cards: Visa, MasterCard, and American Express.
Personal checks: Accepted for deposit only. Not accepted at time of check-in.

QUEEN VICTORIA BED AND BREAKFAST INN

It's poetic justice that the lady whose name is synonymous with the entire Victorian movement also finds her moniker on one of the town's most magnificent inns. The incredible Queen Victoria is one of Cape May's largest B&Bs. The complex contains thirty-two guest rooms and suites scattered among four properties, including perhaps the most luxurious room in any Cape May accommodation—the Crown Jewel Suite, a room so opulent that even Buckingham Palace would be hard-pressed to match it.

The main house was built in 1881 by Douglas Gregory, a Delaware River pilot. It is a Mansard-style building with Italianate detailing and has perhaps the best example of the mansard-type roof in Cape May. The inn actually consists of two buildings with thirty-two guest rooms, the main house and the adjacent Prince Albert Hall.

Congenial hosts Doug and Anna Marie McMain turned to innkeeping after years of success in the computer field. Bits and bytes can't compete with tea and gingerbread, and the two were soon in the market for a B&B to fulfill their lifelong dream of becoming innkeepers. It was only natural that the dream become a reality in the bed-and-breakfast capital of the East Coast. About the change from computers to innkeeping, Anna Marie says, "We love it. It's less stressful, and we truly enjoy being with the guests."

Just a block away from both the Washington Street Mall and the Atlantic Ocean, the Queen Victoria is perfectly located. The building is an impressive structure. It dominates the corner it sits on, dwarfing all surrounding buildings. With its distinctive muted gray-green outside color with red shingles, it's as familiar a sight in Cape May as the horse-drawn carriages. A green, wrought-iron fence with red tips surrounds the property.

The inn offers four different types of rooms—standard, large standard, large premium, and luxury suites—as well as the Regents Park Suite and Crown Jewel Suite. All rooms have a private bath, television, minirefrigerator, hair dryer, clock radio, iron and ironing board, and air-conditioning. The inn provides the free use of bicycles for its guests.

Visiting the Queen Victoria Bed and Breakfast Inn

102 Ocean St., Cape May, NJ 08204
Telephone: 609-884-8702
Website: www.queenvictoria.com • E-mail: stay@queenvictoria.com

Season: Open year-round.
Rooms: 32 guest rooms.
Handicap access: Limited; Regent's Park Cottage has some access.
Parking: Off-site.
Credit cards: MasterCard, Visa, and Discover.
Personal checks: Accepted.
Other: Member of Select Registry.

The Queen Victoria Bed and Breakfast occupies a prominent location in the midst of the Historic District. QUEEN VICTORIA B&B

The standard rooms contain queen beds and a European-style hydro-massage shower. The large standard rooms have more space and chairs or settees along with the queen beds. All have an adjustable hydro-massage shower; some have an old-fashioned claw-foot tub. The large premium rooms and all suites contain luxury baths with whirlpool tubs, and some have a gas-log fireplace.

All of this is leading up to the unbelievably opulent two-story Crown Jewel, where *Luxury* is spelled with a capital *L*. It is the most lavish room in all of Cape May, a place where Queen Victoria herself would be comfortable.

The bottom floor, known as the Library, contains a leather Chesterfield couch, gas-log fireplace, forty-two-inch high-definition television with DVD, Bose surround sound system, telephone, butler's pantry with wet bar, stocked refrigerator, Flavia gourmet coffee system, and microwave. The private first-floor bathroom has a glass-enclosed shower for two, with dual massaging shower heads, and is equipped with a professional lighted magnified makeup mirror.

A staircase takes you to a Juliet balcony and second-floor sleeping loft with a two-person marble-surrounded whirlpool tub, gas Franklin stove, king-size pillow-top bed, color television, Bose Wave CD player and radio, telephone, and sitting area with antique appointments. All of this comes with personal climate control, a private entrance, private patio, and adjacent on-site parking.

As can be gleaned from this description, the Crown Jewel is extraordinarily luxurious. The dwelling sits just a few feet from the main building, giving Crown Jewel guests the feeling of being in solitude, even though the main house is so close they could practically reach out and touch it.

The Queen Victoria also treats its guests royally when it comes to food. *The Queen Victoria Cookbook* contains more than eighty of the recipes that have made the inn a culinary landmark over the years. It is divided into sections, including "Breakfast Main Dishes," "Fruits and Jams," and "Holiday and House Specialties." One thing not to miss, no matter what the time of day, is the Queen's Oats, the inn's famous granola cereal.

"People love the attention to detail here," says Doug. "Everything has been thought of for them. This is the queen of the inns."

VICTORIAN LACE INN

Carrie and Andy O'Sullivan always loved the bed-and-breakfast lifestyle. So when the opportunity presented itself for the couple to become innkeepers in the nation's leading bed-and-breakfast resort, they jumped at the chance. The result is an inn infused with grace, warmth, and homey hospitality just one block from the beach.

The Victorian Lace has an interesting history. Built as a summer home for a Philadelphia couple around 1900, the house actually started out as a Queen Anne Victorian. During the course of construction, it was altered to its present Colonial Revival style. The result is larger rooms and a lighter, airier feel than many of its Cape May counterparts. It's also unusual in that it has cedar shingles. Indeed, the house would actually fit in well in New England. The Victorian Lace has another feature unique to Colonial Revival homes, and possibly unique to Cape

The Victorian Lace Inn stands out as mix of architectural styles. VICTORIAN LACE INN

May—a chimney staircase, which provides excellent ventilation throughout the entire residence.

The house is much larger than many of Cape May's Victorian B&Bs. Seeing it from the outside for the first time, all alone on its corner lot (many of the town's Victorians are squeezed shoulder-to-shoulder like clothes in a crowded closet), with its unique double-decker front porches, you still don't get a sense of how truly large this inn is. It's only when you get inside and experience the sense of space that the large size can truly be appreciated.

In their previous lives, Andy was an architect and engineer, and Carrie worked in human services. Architecture and human services' loss is Cape May's gain. The Victorian Lace is an exceptionally hospitable inn, reflecting the personalities of the O'Sullivans. It's as if you've walked into their house—and indeed, they live on the premises. "We're very laid-back," says Carrie. "This is home for us. We're not real formal people."

Another thing that makes the Victorian Lace atypical is that most of its rooms are suites. The inn has three suites, one guest room, and a carriage house. Two of the suites can become two-bedroom suites if necessary. Each has its own living room, kitchenette, and private bath. The freedom that the living room and kitchen provide is one of the main reasons the couple purchased this inn.

Upon acquiring the inn, the couple performed numerous renovations, including installing central heat and air-conditioning and putting fireplaces in all the suites. They also restored the inn's porch to its previous appearance before storms destroyed it. Today the wraparound porch with its clustered columns is one of the highlights of the Victorian Lace. Guests usually discover its charm early in their visit and don't abandon it until the hour of their departure.

Visiting the Victorian Lace Inn

901 Stockton Ave., Cape May, NJ 08204
Telephone: 609-884-1772
Website: www.victorianlaceinn.com
E-mail: innkeeper@VictorianLaceInn.com

Season: Mid-February through December.
Rooms: Four suites, one guest room, and a carriage house.
Handicap access: No.
Parking: On-site parking for suites only.
Credit cards: Accepted.
Personal checks: Inquire.

The Victorian Lace Inn provides a welcoming atmosphere. VICTORIAN LACE INN

The O'Sullivans prepare a peach French toast for breakfast that guests not only rave over, but set their schedules by. "People will come and say, 'You're having the French toast, aren't you?'" says Carrie with a laugh.

Many Cape May inns do not allow kids under ten or twelve, but the Victorian Lace welcomes children. "We enjoy having them," says Andy. Kids enjoy the inn's laid-back atmosphere and also enjoy J. J., the O'Sullivans' golden retriever, which is the house's community dog. The child-friendly environment includes a side yard with a picnic area and barbecue grill that is open to all.

The O'Sullivans also own the Cape May Day Spa, which allows them to offer special spa packages in conjunction with a stay at the Victorian Lace. "It's great for couples," notes Andy.

A stay at the Victorian Lace gives you the feeling that you're among friends. The O'Sullivans wouldn't have it any other way. "We enjoy meeting new people and having guests in our home," says Carrie. "We've made some really wonderful friends. We like the idea that when people leave here, they're leaving friends."

WHITE DOVE COTTAGE

Filled with amazing collections from the eighteenth century and Victorian era, the White Dove Cottage is a collector's and antique lover's dream. There is no common theme, no underlying deep meaning, but everything fits together to provide an inn of unparalleled beauty and grace.

The White Dove was constructed in 1866 as a summer home for a Philadelphia innkeeper. It was built in the Second Empire style, with a mansard roof still faced with the original octagonal slate tiles, making it one of the oldest original roofs in Cape May. The house has had several other careers over its lifetime, including serving at one point as a weather station.

Mother-daughter innkeeping team Alison and Joan Bjork have turned their lifetime love of old houses and antiques into one of Cape May's most pleasant inns. "We're both antique collectors, and innkeeping just seemed like something we could do together," says Joan.

Visiting the White Dove Cottage

619 Hughes St., Cape May, NJ 08204
Telephone: 609-884-0613 or 800-321-DOVE
Website: www.whitedovecottage.com

Season: Open year-round.
Rooms: 6 guest rooms.
Handicap access: No.
Parking: On-site.
Credit cards: Not accepted.
Personal checks: Accepted.

The White Dove has six guest rooms, of which two are suites. Each room has a private bath as well as a TV with VCR, ceiling fan, room safe, hair dryer, and air-conditioning in the summer and heat in the winter. The suites each have a TV with VCR in the private sitting room with love seat, a fireplace in winter, and air-conditioning in the summer. The Lady Kathy Suite has an optional two-person Jacuzzi.

Although the White Dove has its fair share of amenities, such as towels and chairs for beachgoers, what catches the attention of most guests is the decor. "A lot of people like the decor," says Joan. "It's not strict Victorian; it's a little brighter than that. It's probably more Colonial than Victorian."

Collections at the White Dove include Currier and Ives prints, oil paintings, equestrian art, and quilts. Perhaps the most unusual is a collection of Victorian blue milk glass. The objects are set all about the inn and immediately draw the eye with their striking color.

The White Dove serves a full sit-down breakfast that includes a variety of hot entrees, juices, fruits, home-baked breads, desserts, coffee, and teas. The Bjorks accommodate any special dietary need. The two women make it a point to be around at breakfast time to help guests plan their day, if necessary. They find that most guests like their being available then.

Situated in the heart of the Historic District, just two blocks from the pedestrian mall and two blocks from the beach, the front porch of the White Dove is a popular gathering place, particularly during the summer. "The guests go out there, drink a bottle of wine, and just relax," says Joan. "They just want to relax, and we're happy that they can find such peace here."

PET FRIENDLY CAPE MAY BED-AND-BREAKFASTS

Billmae Cottage
1015 Washington St., Cape May, NJ 08204
Telephone: 609-898-8558
Website: www.billmae.com

Highland House
131 North Broadway, West Cape May, NJ 08204
Telephone: 609-898-1198
Website: www.highlandhousecapemay.com
E-mail: HighlandHouseCapeMay@mail.com

Other Accommodations

ATLAS INN

The Atlas Inn is exactly the type of large, spacious, family-friendly inn that you'd like to find in Cape May but thought didn't exist there. Not only is the motel itself great for families and large groups, but its restaurant, Yesterday's Heroes, has the most incredible collection of baseball memorabilia this side of Cooperstown–including a life-size, animatronic Babe Ruth.

The Atlas Inn features ninety rooms and suites. Each room has a coffeemaker, refrigerator, hair dryer, telephone with voice mail and dataport, cable television, and individual heating and air-conditioning controls. The efficiency suites also have microwaves. Although no room is 100 percent handicap accessible, each bathroom provides sturdy grab bars, and one has an extrawide doorway and additional grab bars by the toilet.

Rooms at the Atlas are surprisingly large. Many offer comfortable couches in the living-room area, which is sufficiently separate from the sleeping quarters that activities in one do not have to be heard in the other.

The hotel also contains numerous amenities, including an exercise room, coin laundry, barbecue grills, sundeck, complimentary breakfast, free local phone calls and daily newspaper, and oceanfront balconies. It is located right across the street from the ocean. There is a very large parking lot behind the hotel.

The Atlas has both side- and ocean-view rooms. The view from your window of the sun rising over the ocean is truly spectacular. Although it's your vacation, and hence it's your God-given right to sleep late, watching the rising sun–glistening off the ocean as it slowly rises in the dawn sky–from a room at the Atlas is highly recommended.

The Atlas offers a special Reunion Package, which includes a welcome reception at Yesterday's Heroes, breakfast, dinner one night or a choice of several different excursions, and a reunion dinner dance. Thus the Atlas has become the unofficial home of many Cape May reunion groups, from veterans to school chums. Other packages include golf, wedding weekends, and holidays.

The inn also offers various tours for groups of twenty-five or more throughout the year. The tours visit sites specific to the tour topic and provide dining arrangements. Among them are the Nostalgia Tour, Lighthouse and Lobster Tour, Gourmet Cape May Tour, and Fall in Love Tour.

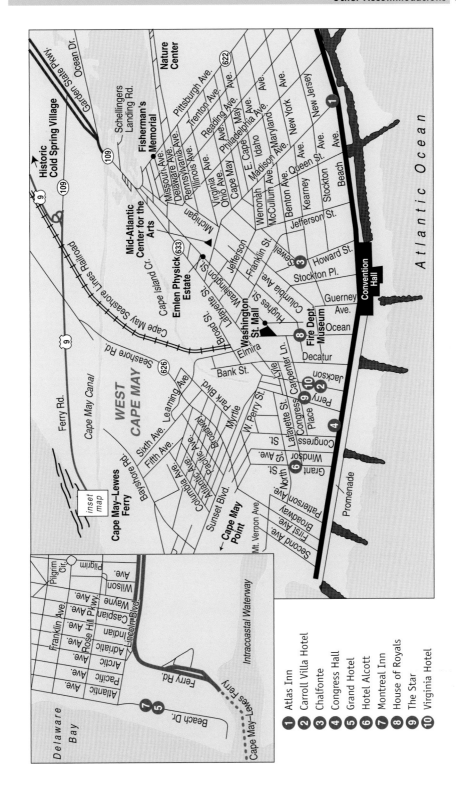

1 Atlas Inn
2 Carroll Villa Hotel
3 Chalfonte
4 Congress Hall
5 Grand Hotel
6 Hotel Alcott
7 Montreal Inn
8 House of Royals
9 The Star
10 Virginia Hotel

Visiting the Atlas Inn

1035 Beach Ave., Cape May, NJ 08204
Telephone: 609-884-7000 or 888-285-2746
Fax: 609-884-0301
Website: www.atlasinn.com • E-Mail: atlasinn@msn.com

Season: Early April through December.
Rooms: 90 guest rooms.
Handicap access: One room is accessible.
Parking: On-site.
Credit cards: Accepted.
Personal checks: Accepted for initial deposit only.

Although the Atlas is directly across the street from the beach, it is close enough to the downtown shopping areas that you can easily reach them by bicycle, especially if you cut through the back streets of the Historic District. It is also very near the stores and businesses along Beach Drive, as well as a movie theater right across from Convention Hall that is perfect for kids during the season and can be reached by walking.

Above all, the Atlas is a big hotel-type facility of the kind that most people do not know exists in Cape May. Informal, attractive, neat, and well situated, the Atlas is the perfect place for families to stay.

The family-friendly Atlas is located across the street from the beach. PAT KING-ROBERTS

CARROLL VILLA HOTEL

The Carroll Villa has been in the Kulkowitz family for about thirty years. During that time, the hotel has seen Cape May rise from the ashes of a nondescript summer resort to become the bed-and-breakfast capital of the world. That rise has been helped along by the consistent excellence of the Carroll Villa Hotel and its restaurant, the famed Mad Batter.

In a city known for Victoriana, the Carroll Villa is one of a vanishing breed in Cape May—the Victorian hotel. Built in 1882 as a seaside escape for families, the Carroll Villa building is in the Italian Villa or American Bracketed Villa architectural style. It features a sweeping porch, tall front windows, and a symmetrical facade. The building is a national historic landmark. As was true of the seaside villas of that time, the Carroll Villa rooms were spare and austere. When bathrooms were added, they were down the hall, two to a floor. There was a common parlor for socializing and a large dining room for meals.

For nearly 100 years, the Carroll Villa watched the rise, fall, and rise of Cape May. But no matter how Cape May changed, the hotel enjoyed a reputation for quality. When the Kulkowitz family purchased the Carroll Villa in 1978, however, the hotel was clearly showing its age. The thirty-one rooms were painted in dark colors, and each had an odd combination of a beautiful antique dresser and a rather worn-out iron bedstead. There were many connecting doors between the rooms, and the hotel had only eight bathrooms. Though historic, the Carroll Villa was a restoration project waiting to happen.

The Kulkowitzes rolled up their sleeves and got to work. The biggest problem was reconfiguring the size of each room to provide today's guests the amenities they expect, including private bathrooms. When the dust cleared, the Carroll Villa had twenty-two Victorian guest rooms, all beautifully furnished with period antiques. Each also had a private bath, ceiling fan, phones, and air-conditioning.

Guests receive a full hot breakfast—including such things as Eggs Benedict, French toast, Belgian waffles, and fresh-squeezed juices—downstairs at the Mad Batter restaurant at no extra charge. And if Carroll Villa guests wish to eat dinner at the Mad Batter, they receive a voucher for 30 percent off the total dinner bill with the

Visiting the Carroll Villa Hotel

19 Jackson St., Cape May, NJ 08204
Telephone: 877-275-8452
Website: www.carrollvilla.com • E-mail: manager@carrollvilla.com

Season: Open year-round.
Rooms: 22 guest rooms.
Handicap access: No.
Parking: On-site, May through October.
Credit cards: Visa, MasterCard, American Express, and Discover.
Personal checks: Accepted for deposit only.

purchase of at least two adult entrees. It's extras like these that have made the Carroll Villa one of the consistently excellent hotels in Cape May.

Owner Mark Kulkowitz credits the Jackson Street location with a portion of his hotel's popularity. This is one of the oldest streets in America, and it attracts tourists throughout the year, who wander up and down the tree-lined avenue just to soak in the atmosphere. At the Carroll Villa, you can sit on the wide, comfortable front porch, sipping a cocktail and watching the passing parade go by on historic Jackson Street.

The Carroll Villa's location also places it in a prime position as far as Cape May's activities go. The hotel is just a stone's throw from the beach and a few blocks from the Washington Street Mall. It is also fairly close to the shops on Beach Drive, the Beach Drive movie theater, Convention Hall, and numerous restaurants. As central locations go, there are few better in Cape May.

Like the House of Royals, the Carroll Villa is not set up like a modern hotel with a prominent check-in office. Rather, it shares stairs and an entrance with the Mad Batter, which is located on the bottom floor front and is the more prominent outside structure. If you travel up and down Jackson Street and miss the hotel sign, just look for the Mad Batter.

Location wouldn't mean anything without a memorable stay to back it up, and here the Carroll Villa has been delivering the goods for years. Mark gets a kick out of welcoming the children and grandchildren of guests who first came to the Carroll Villa three decades ago, which demonstrates the enduring popularity of the establishment. Those who stayed here as children are now coming back as adults to relive those long-ago memories. The hotel has a well-established international reputation, and guests come here from as far away as Europe, Australia, and Vietnam.

Mark would like the hotel to be known for several things: food, hospitality, and accommodating staff. Above all, he just wants his guests to enjoy a nice stay. "I want this to be a nice break from their daily lives," he says.

As they say in Australia, "No worries, mate."

CHALFONTE

Suffice it to say that there is nothing else like the Chalfonte in all of Cape May. In fact, there may be nothing else like the Chalfonte on the entire East Coast.

Innkeepers often say that they're trying to create a friendly atmosphere and deliver the feel of relaxed nineteenth-century living. The Chalfonte really does it. The hotel does not have televisions, telephones, heat or air-conditioning; and most rooms do not have private baths. Instead, what the Chalfonte does have is a unique atmosphere that is second to none. It is built on the ancient arts of friendship, civility, courtesy, and face-to-face conversation. This also is one of Cape May's most popular hotels, and some of its recipes have appeared in books and on television and have spawned a cookbook of their own.

The hotel was built in 1876 by Col. Henry Sawyer, a Union Army war hero during the Civil War known for his involvement with the famous "lottery of death." Sawyer, taken prisoner in 1863 at the Battle of Brandy Station, was selected by lot-

Visiting the Chalfonte Hotel

301 Howard St., Cape May, NJ 08204
Telephone: 609-884-8409 or 888-411-1998
Fax: 609-884-4588 • Website: www.chalfonte.com
E-mail: info@chalfonte.com or reservations@chalfonte.com

Season: Memorial Day through Columbus Day.
Rooms: 70 guest rooms, 13 with private bath; 27 types of rooms.
Handicap access: A wheelchair-accessible ramp enters the hotel. Two guest rooms are completely accessible; they share an accessible bathroom with a rolling shower.
Parking: On-street.
Credit cards: Inquire.
Personal checks: Inquire.
Other: The hotel requests that guests dress for dinner.

tery to be executed in retaliation for the killings of two Southern colonels. Mrs. Sawyer hurried to Washington, D.C., and got a personal audience with the compassionate president Lincoln, who agreed to help. Lincoln ordered that if Sawyer or anyone else were summarily executed, he would order the execution of two Southern captives. The South, realizing that it was about to ignite a never-ending retaliation contest, backed down and did not follow through with the execution of Sawyer.

The Chalfonte stays true to its nineteenth-century heritage. CHALFONTE

The Chalfonte's Magnolia Dining Room, where Dot's Southern Fried Chicken is the signature dish. CHALFONTE

On returning to Cape May after the war, Sawyer looked around, saw the trend in town turning away from hotels and toward cottages, and built . . . a hotel. The hotel and an addition two years later were a significant improvement in architectural refinement over the pre–Civil War Cape May hotels. Though it was in no way extravagant, the building had a simple, dignified Italian form—sometimes known as Cube Italian in Cape May—with a balanced plan and façade.

Sawyer sold the hotel in 1888. Until it was bought by the Satterfield family of Richmond, Virginia, in 1911, the hotel had several owners. One extended the Chalfonte to its current size, adding another twenty-three rooms, enlarging the dining room, and providing architectural riddles for future preservationists to solve. Where the two phases of construction join, one cannot discern a serious effort to marry the disparate architectural and building styles. This is seen in the change of hotel room size and configuration, with the addition of some private baths, and in the randomness of the construction in the last addition, which contrasts directly with the carefully orchestrated details of Sawyer's construction, as evidenced by changes in roof and ceiling, variations in flooring type in the dining room, abrupt cessation of crown molding in the dining room, and a change in board wainscot in the dining room.

The Chalfonte is easy to find. It sprawls over a complete block, with its white exterior and green trim and its giant front porch. Inside, the building is surprisingly cool, even on the hottest days, but the real pleasure is in the people. They are unfailingly polite—both guests and staff—and say "please" and "thank you" so much that you'll feel you've stumbled into an English comedy of manners. But it's no joke: Civility reigns at the Chalfonte.

Current owner Anne LeDuc has run the hotel since 1983. She has never been tempted to install modern devices such as telephones or televisions, says Debra Donahue, public relations director. "She saw the hotel as a way to maintain values of friendship, camaraderie, and conversation."

Because of the hotel's singular throwback status, it has perhaps the most fiercely loyal clientele anywhere. It lacks heat and air-conditioning, so the Chalfonte is only open seasonally, from about Memorial Day to Columbus Day. People rearrange their lives and schedules to ensure that they can stay at the Chalfonte, rock on the wide columned front porch constantly buffeted by cool sea breezes (the ocean is a few blocks away), and discuss a wide range of topics with their neighbors. The hotel is now welcoming its third and fourth generation of guests. This trend applies to the staff as well.

The Chalfonte specializes in southern cooking in the Magnolia Dining Room. In particular, Dot's Southern Fried Chicken is the hotel's signature dish. Featured in both the print and electronic media, it has been named one of the top-ten fried chicken recipes in America. A typical breakfast may include, besides the usual morning fare, chicken, hash, grits, fried flounder, and spoon bread. Sundays feature a southern buffet, including fried and baked chicken, Virginia ham, black-eyed peas, stewed tomatoes, and corn pudding.

The hotel's two cooks, Lucille and Dot, have published a cookbook titled *I Just Quit Stirrin' When the Tastin's Good* and are real characters. To truly appreciate their witty repartee and playfulness, you have to take the Food and Wine Tour, which ends up in the Chalfonte's kitchen. But make no mistake about it—these two gracious ladies know their stuff. The food at the Chalfonte is delicious.

Rooms at the hotel are simple yet elegant. Each is furnished with a marble-topped dresser and washstand, ceiling fan, and outer louvered door (think dressing-room-type shutter) to usher in the cool ocean breezes. The louvered door can be locked, allowing the inner door to remain open, thus letting the breeze circulate around the room. Most of the room furniture is original.

The Chalfonte also offers the Franklin Street Cottage. There's no air-conditioning here either, but the twenty-first century—or at least the twentieth—makes its appearance in the form of a TV with VCR, refrigerator, stove, and microwave oven. The single standing cottage sleeps a maximum of eight people, with four bedrooms, two bathrooms, a nice-size family room, and a wraparound porch.

"The culture of the hotel is driven by the people who come here," says Debra Donahue. "People get here what they cannot get anywhere else. There is something magical about this place. This kind of place—rocking chairs and reverence for quiet—still exists."

CONGRESS HALL

Beach Drive is filled with excellent hotels and inns. Yet none is more imposing or luxurious than Congress Hall, a magnificent, white-columned structure that dominates Beach Drive like the Empire State Building dominates Manhattan Island.

When Congress Hall was first built in 1816, it was one of the largest hotels in America. This was long before vacationing at the shore was a popular, or even accepted, thing to do. So the idea of building a gigantic boardinghouse, as it was first known, at the seashore was considered not only novel, but insane. The owner, Thomas H. Hughes, didn't much care what people thought, however. He proudly called his Spartan retreat, which when first built had neither plaster nor paint, the Big House. But the locals took one look at this monstrous-size building and promptly dubbed it Tommy's Folly.

Nevertheless, Hughes had seen the magnificent Atlantic Ocean shimmering in the sunlight just beyond his massive front lawn and knew he was onto something big. Travelers kept coming to the hotel, even though its notoriously unreliable supply of provisions could run out at any time. Even an 1818 fire that destroyed the hotel didn't put a crimp in Hughes's confidence. He just rebuilt, bigger and better. By the time he sold it in 1826, Hughes's vision had been justified by the constantly growing streams of visitors.

Congress Hall is one of Cape May's largest and most luxurious properties. CONGRESS HALL

In 1829, the new owners changed the name to Congress Hall in honor of Hughes's election to Congress, but by that time, they could have called the building Harry's Horse Apple Hotel and it wouldn't have mattered. As Cape May grew and prospered as one of the premier resort towns in the United States, Congress Hall grew right along with it.

In the summer of 1891, when President Benjamin Harrison had to leave the White House because of renovations, he stayed at Congress Hall for four months and established the concept of the Summer White House. (Harrison had electricity installed in the White House, but suspicious of it, he never turned on the lights. He left that job to his successor, Grover Cleveland.)

March king John Philip Sousa loved Congress Hall so much that after playing concerts on the front lawn, he composed a march in the hotel's honor: "Congress Hall March." On July 4, 2004, it was played for the first time since 1882.

It took the ultimate destructive power of the Great Depression to bring Congress Hall to its knees. For the next sixty years, the hotel remained in a twilight zone of its former glory, including an almost thirty-year stint from 1968 to 1995 as part of the Cape May Bible Conference under Rev. Carl McIntire. This use of the hotel during that period

Congress Hall reopened in 2002 after undergoing a massive renovation. CONGRESS HALL

One of the newly refurbished rooms at Congress Hall. CONGRESS HALL

almost certainly saved the building from demolition.

In 1995, the current owners bought the hotel and launched a $25 million renovation project with the idea of restoring Congress Hall to its former glory . . . and have they ever succeeded. The new Congress Hotel, opened in 2002, is the epitome of class and style in Cape May.

"We've had four presidents stay with us—Pierce, Buchanan, Grant, and Harrison," notes Congress Hall's pleasant and extraordinarily knowledgeable concierge, Bill Briggs. He is an incredible font of information on Congress Hall's past, present, and future. The amount of information he casually offers on a tour around the facility is staggering. Little wonder that his Saturday morning tours of Congress Hall are wildly popular. History class in school was never this interesting.

The building drips uniqueness and luxury. Its singular style is reflected in the two gigantic wooden soldiers that stand guard at the front entrance, its restaurant called the Blue Pig, and its basement rip-up-the-night dance club, the Boiler Room—which, incidentally, once was a boiler room.

Inside, Congress Hall is wood-paneled sleekness, muted light softness, and quirky corners—reflecting the builders of another era, who didn't feel obligated to make every corner straight and angle true. From its comfortable front lobby with soft chairs to its offices scattered along the bottom hallway, Congress Hall is quiet, mellow, dignified—and wonderful.

The one thing Bill wants Congress Hall to be known for is hospitality, and he has no worries on that score. The general hotel amenities are many in number.

Visiting Congress Hall

251 Beach Ave., Cape May, NJ 08204
Telephone: 609-884-8421 or 888-944-1816
Website: www.congresshall.com • E-mail: congress@congresshall.com

Season: Open year-round.
Rooms: 104 guest rooms.
Handicap access: A few rooms are ADA compliant. Ramps at some hotel entrances.
Parking: Valet and private.
Credit cards: Accepted.
Personal checks: Inquire.

They include on-site and valet parking, a cocktail lounge, night club, 106 newly renovated guest rooms, five luxury suites, a fitness room, a full-service spa called the Cape May Day Spa, and lobby shopping. The centerpiece of the hotel is a 400-square-foot ballroom.

Congress Hall offers four distinct room types: premium, deluxe, luxurious suites, and connecting rooms, which are perfect for families. Each room has a private bathroom, individual climate control, cable flat-screen television with a DVD player, a CD player with an alarm clock, a daily newspaper, two telephones, voice mail, and a dataport.

The deluxe rooms have more space. Many contain a king-size bed or a larger bathroom with a separate soaking tub and tiled shower. Luxurious suites have private balconies with views over the veranda and lawns to the sea.

Beyond all this is the atmosphere that Congress Hall projects. It is a feeling of old-time luxury mixed with modern amenities. It is a feeling of unbridled splendor and elegance found in every nook and cranny of the hotel, from the desk clerk's cheery smile to the star logo that appears everywhere. It is a feeling that every whim and whimsy of a guest is going to be fulfilled.

"If you want something, I'm going to get it for you," says Bill.

GRAND HOTEL

Quick! What's the largest full-service hotel and convention center south of Atlantic City? If you said Cape May's Grand Hotel, go to the head of the accommodations class.

The hotel got its start in the 1950s as the Golden Eagle. After several additions, it became the Grand in the 1980s. Today it is one massive facility. The sprawling structure has 165 guest rooms. It also has fifteen meeting rooms and two ballrooms that can be customized to fit business needs.

The Grand Hotel is in the shape of a U, with the opening pointing toward the beach across the street. The rooms on the top floor of the right side of the U as it faces the beach have a spectacular, unencumbered view of the sand and water, as well as the ocean horizon.

Inside, the Grand Hotel is elegant and cool. The styling, perhaps befitting the U shape, is long and lean rather than round and squat. The entrance corridor is elegant, with numerous places to sit and relax before checking in and taking the elevator to your room.

The amenities include refrigerators in each room, banquet facilities, beauty salon, coin laundry, restaurant, game room, phone and fax service, three sundecks, indoor whirlpool and heated pool, and outdoor heated adult and kiddie pools. The indoor pool is quite large—much bigger than the outside one—and is graced by a large mural on one wall of people walking on a beach. The atmosphere is at once both nostalgic and relaxing. On-site parking is also provided for one car per unit, either inside the U or in a covered parking garage. Families on a budget will appreciate the rooms that come equipped with everything for light cooking: range top, dishes, cookware, toaster, and microwave, in addition to the refrigerator.

The sprawling Grand Hotel is the largest hotel in Cape May. PAT KING-ROBERTS

The rooms are spacious, and six are completely handicap accessible. Many have a balcony where you can sit in pleasant weather and enjoy a late-night snack or just take in the air. An unusual feature of the Grand is its large, two-story, open-air courtyard overlooking the beach, where you also can sit or stroll in nice weather.

The Grand Hotel is open year-round. It has a multitiered pricing structure for each room, depending on the type of room and time of year. See the hotel's website for a complete listing.

The Grand has an on-site restaurant called Ballyhoos, which features American cuisine. The wallet-stretching, all-you-can-eat breakfast buffet is popular

Visiting the Grand Hotel

1045 Beach Dr., Cape May, NJ 08204
Telephone: 609-884-5611 or 800-257-8550
Website: www.grandhotelcapemay.com
E-mail: info@grandhotelcapemay.com

Season: Open year-round.
Rooms: 165 guest rooms.
Handicap access: 6 rooms are accessible.
Parking: On-site.
Credit cards: All major credit cards accepted.
Personal checks: Not accepted.

with guests and locals alike. For dinner, Thursday night has an all-you-can-eat seafood extravaganza.

For all these reasons and more, the Grand Hotel is extremely popular with families. Groups also flock to the Grand, because it has the physical size and facilities to accommodate the largest groups and is open even when the rest of Cape May slumbers. The Grand's general manager, Bob Belansen Jr., says that the hotel can arrange comprehensive packages for tour groups, including food and beverage in the hotel, plus entertainment.

The hotel also offers numerous weekend and holiday specials. Among these are the Grand Rhapsody Weekends and the very popular Guest Appreciation Weekends.

For a grand time in Cape May, it's hard to beat the Grand Hotel.

HOTEL ALCOTT

Built in 1878, this hotel started life as the Arlington House. But then it became the favorite hotel of a certain female author, who stayed there on a regular basis, and soon the Arlington House was renamed the Hotel Alcott.

Another Victorian-era gem, the Hotel Alcott, is the second-oldest operating hotel in Cape May. At one point, the Cape May railroad station was across the street, which is the reason for the hotel's location. The architectural style of the building is Italianate Bracketed Villa, emphasized today even more so because of an extensive restoration that preserved the hotel's architectural integrity while bringing

The Hotel Alcott is one of the architectural gems of Cape May. PAT KING-ROBERTS

Visiting the Hotel Alcott

107–113 Grant St., Cape May, NJ 08204
Telephone: 609-884-5868 or 800-272-3004
Website: www.hotelalcott.com

Season: March through December.
Rooms: 31 guest rooms.
Handicap access: One room is accessible.
Parking: Off-site.
Credit cards: Major credit cards accepted.
Personal checks: Accepted for deposit only, if received four weeks before arrival or within seven days of original booking.

it into the modern era. Among the items of architectural significance here are the original hotel dining room, solid chestnut wood in the lobby, plaster ceiling medallions in the lobby, and especially the wide hanging staircase, one of the earliest of its type in this country, featuring no posts or visible supports.

"I took over in 1997," says owner Nick Nezaj. "I really enjoy this business. You deal with a lot of really great people. Being in Cape May, next to the ocean . . . you can't beat it."

When Nick took over, the hotel had more than fifty rooms. He initiated the major overhaul, which produced the combination of a charming and graceful older Victorian hotel with all the amenities of a modern facility that guests enjoy today. The major improvement was in the size of the rooms. Nick turned the original fifty-plus rooms into thirty-one little slices of Victorian heaven, with private tile or granite bathrooms–something that would have turned Louisa May into an even bigger fan, no doubt.

Each of the Alcott's rooms contain amenities such as wireless Internet, an LCD plasma television, individually controlled air-conditioning or heat, concierge service, either a king- or queen-size bed, beach towels, beach tags, and complimentary local telephone calls. The airy veranda is a favorite guest spot, as is the large front porch filled with rocking chairs and the center courtyard with a beautiful fountain. Indeed, courtyard seats are at a premium when the weather is temperate, and there's nothing finer than sitting around the gurgling waters and talking, reading, or just drinking in the joy of doing nothing.

The hotel's restaurant, La Verandah, is another bonus for guests. Recently rated three stars, La Verandah specializes in seafood dishes. It offers a dinner buffet or a grill menu.

The Alcott's front lobby is stunning in its beauty. Chandeliers and potted greenery abound. But what you notice most is the airy sense of space. It's the type of place where Louisa May Alcott herself could have sat in a comfortable chair and written *Little Women* in perfect peace, while all around her guests came and went. Never once would she have been disturbed. It's that spacious.

Nick tries to do something to the hotel every year to keep it in tip-top shape, whether it's remodeling the rooms or common areas or upgrading the bathrooms. The hotel closes for the season after Christmas, and Nick is soon hard at work.

"These older buildings need a lot of TLC," Nick says. "We are always on the look-out to do whatever is necessary to keep the hotel both attractive and responsive to guest's needs." It is this meticulous attention to detail that has made the Hotel Alcott a perennial favorite among Cape May guests.

Old-time Cape May charm with the sophistication for today's travelers: That's the recipe for the Hotel Alcott's success.

MONTREAL INN

For more than forty years, the Montreal Inn has been one of the premier places for families and groups to go in Cape May, and according to marketing director Marcia Palmer, that's not about to change. "We have people returning here year after year," she says. "People bring their kids, and their kids grow up and bring *their* kids."

The Montreal is a seventy-room inn with twenty one-bedroom units and fifty one-bedroom suites. It offers eleven different styles of rooms, including standard motel-type rooms and one-bedroom suites with efficiency kitchens, living rooms, and panoramic three-sided views of the ocean. Some of the rooms can accommodate up to six people.

Located right across the street from the beach, the Montreal has many rooms with an ocean view and a private balcony. In addition, each room has a refrigerator, coffeemaker, television, and microwave. Many rooms are wheelchair accessible, but only two have handicap-accessible bathrooms.

Families enjoy the Montreal not only for its wide variety of rooms and nearby beach location, but also for such features as outdoor heated kiddie and adult pools, two sundecks, a health club and sauna, miniature golf, a game room, and a whirlpool. The Montreal also has its own on-site restaurant, Café Promenade, which serves American cuisine. The inn provides a free airport shuttle from the Cape May Airport.

Along with the Grand Hotel, the Montreal is the hotel of choice for many groups coming to Cape May. "We host a lot of groups," Marcia notes, "especially in the off-season." Many of the groups undoubtedly are attracted by the Montreal's

---

Visiting the Montreal Inn

1025 Beach Ave. (at Madison Ave.), Cape May, NJ 08204
Telephone: 609-884-7011 or 800-525-7011
Fax: 609-884-4559 • Website: www.montreal-inn.com
E-mail: reservations@montreal-inn.com, generalinfo@montreal-inn.com,
or groupinfo@montreal-inn.com

Season: Mid-March through late November.
Rooms: 70 guest rooms.
Handicap access: 2 rooms are accessible.
Parking: On-site.
Credit cards: Discover, American Express, MasterCard, and Visa.
Personal checks: Accepted for deposit only, not for payment of final balance.

ability to arrange tours and meals for everyone. The inn's large parking lot also can accommodate tour buses.

"We call ourselves 'Cape May's most accommodating inn,'" says Marcia, "and it's true. We have so much to offer here that we can usually accommodate anyone's needs, from a couple looking for a weekend getaway to a large tour group looking for planned activities."

HOUSE OF ROYALS

Across the street and right around the corner from the Queen Victoria Bed and Breakfast is the House of Royals, formerly the Queen's Hotel. A companion building to the Queen Victoria, the House of Royals offers eleven rooms for people to experience the Queen Victoria's special touch without staying at the B&B.

Built in 1876 by Charles Shaw, the three-story structure originally housed a drugstore on its bottom floor, a gentlemen's gambling parlor on the second floor, and a series of—ahem—"intimate" bedrooms on the third floor. (Reportedly the ghost of one of the former working girls has been seen there.) The bottom floor remains a store and is the oldest continuously operating storefront in Cape May.

The building was completely gutted and renovated in 1995. The result is a totally modern structure with quirky old-time touches, such as twelve-foot ceilings, eleven-foot doorways, and roomy bathrooms. This unusual scale is one of the things that makes a stay here unique.

From the outside, the building is nothing to look at. It does not stand out and seems to be a part of the overall building on the corner, which also houses some other uses. The front door is on the Columbia Avenue side of the building and is designated by a moderate sign. Those looking for a typical hotel, with a manager's check-in office, are likely to drive past the hotel many times until finally spotting its location.

But that's just part of its charm. The nondescript exterior hides a lavish interior that, as with its sister property across the street, goes the ultimate mile toward making a guest comfortable—even pampered. And the decor here too is rich in Victorian tradition and finery. "It's not exactly your local chain hotel," says proprietor Doug McMain, who runs this property with the same immaculate attention to detail he and his wife, Anna Marie, lavish on the Queen Victoria Bed and Breakfast.

The House of Royals has three different room types: small room, large room, and luxury suite. Some of the rooms are named for the castles that were Queen Victoria's private retreats, Balmoral and Osborne. Each room has Victorian revival wallpaper, ornate window treatments, a queen-size bed, European duvet, luxury marble private bath with whirlpool tub for two or glass-enclosed shower, hair dryer, minirefrigerator, television, heated towel bar, and air-conditioning and heating. Some rooms have a private balcony and ocean view. Hotel amenities include free use of bicycles, beach chairs, beach towels, and wireless high-speed Internet.

"People choose to stay here instead of the bed-and-breakfast because they get a little more privacy," says Doug. But staying here does give them some of the perks of staying at the Queen Victoria. The hotel offers a complimentary European breakfast buffet every day, which includes all of the same baked goods that are available at the

---

Visiting the House of Royals

601 Columbia Ave. (Ocean St. and Columbia Ave.)
Cape May, NJ 08204
Telephone: 609-884-1613 • Website: www.queenshotel.com

Season: Open year-round.
Rooms: 11 guest rooms.
Handicap access: No.
Parking: On-street.
Credit cards: Accepted.
Personal checks: Accepted for deposit only.
Other: Member of Select Registry.

Queen Victoria. And also like the Queen Victoria, the House of Royals offers special package deals, such as the Indulgence Package, which includes a two-night stay in a room with a queen-size bed, an in-room massage, a bouquet of fresh flowers, and a butler's breakfast tray for two delivered to the room both mornings. Lower rates are available Monday through Thursday from early September to mid-June.

The Queen Victoria it's not, but the beautifully modern yet unexpectedly old-fashioned House of Royals is certainly a worthy relative.

THE STAR

OK, so you want to go to Cape May, but you have three young kids. You know it would be a bad idea to take them to a bed-and-breakfast, even one that accepts children, and you're also not so sure about a hotel like Congress Hall. You're in a quandary. What to do?

Fortunately, there is an answer. Pack up that suitcase and get going to the Star.

The Star is located just across the street from Congress Hall and is a sister property of that hotel. The Star is actually three separate properties, all grouped together at the same location: a nine-room inn, nine modern efficiency apartments, and two condominiums. In its twenty rooms, the Star combines the best of the B&B and luxury hotel world with the rugged, live-at-home world. And because it's a member of the Congress Hall family, you get to take advantage of all the amenities that the hotel across the street has to offer, including its large, gorgeous pool and relaxing spa.

The first property is a bed-and-breakfast inn. Many rooms offer an

Spacious rooms are a luxurious feature at the Star. THE STAR

The Star, Congress Hall's "sister" property just across the street. THE STAR

ocean view. All have private bathrooms, TV, and other amenities. There is a convenient coffeeshop on the first floor that is open in the warm-weather months for guests.

The second property has nine efficiency apartments that are just perfect for families. Each unit has two televisions (the one in the bedroom is a VCR-DVD combination unit), a high-speed Internet connection, and a kitchenette consisting of a two-burner stove, a sink, small refrigerator, coffeemaker, and microwave. The units are designed so that the kids can watch TV and commit mayhem in the front room while you relax on the bed in the other room. These rooms are spacious, airy, neat, and clean. First-floor rooms have private backyards, and each second-floor room has a small outside sitting area.

The third property is the Carriage House Suites, which has two condominiums each with two bedrooms and two bathrooms, a full kitchen in lieu of a kitchenette, a full living area, and a full-length outside deck. Each also contains a pull-out sofabed, so you can fit up to six people in it. Like the efficiencies, these units are ideal for families.

The Star is a short half block from the beach. It's also only two blocks from downtown Cape May, so it's close to all the shopping areas and some restaurants. The property has its own private parking lot, which means that you can just park the car when you arrive and not worry about it again until departure.

Like Congress Hall, the Star is high on the list of desirable Cape May lodging.

Visiting the Star Inn

29 Perry St., Cape May, NJ 08204
Telephone: 609-884-4590 or 800-297-3779
Website: www.thestarinn.net • E-mail: starinn@thestarinn.net

Season: Open year-round.
Rooms: 20 guest rooms.
Handicap access: One of the Carriage House suites is accessible.
Parking: On-site.
Credit cards: Accepted.
Personal checks: Inquire.

VIRGINIA HOTEL

The Virginia is a recently renovated Victorian-looking hotel that inside is actually much more European in style and decor. Combined with its fabulous restaurant, the Ebbitt Room, this is one of Cape May's finest establishments.

In 1879, Alfred and Ellen Ebbitt built a small but elegant hotel called the Virginia on Jackson Street. Today, with its twenty-four newly renovated guest rooms, the Virginia Hotel maintains the Ebbitts' tradition of quality accommodations and service. The hotel has received numerous accolades as one of the very best in town.

The Virginia is often described as a "boutique hotel," and Eric Greenberg, the property's marketing manager, says he would agree with that assessment. "The Virginia is a smaller hotel with wide-open, airy interiors, like those found in Europe," he says. Eric explains that the hotel avoids the dark, crowded feeling common to some Victorian interiors. Instead, with its use of bright colors, plenty of greenery, and funky touches like red-and-white-striped lampshades, the Virginia resembles a hotel in Paris or Vienna.

Having just undergone a renovation in 2005, the hotel is perfectly equipped for the modern traveler. Both the common areas and the guest rooms are large and bright, with thick, soft carpets and inviting furniture. Each room has custom furnishings, a down comforter, private bathroom, in-room minibar, plasma TV with DVD, and wireless high-speed Internet access. In addition, a few rooms have private porches overlooking historic Jackson Street.

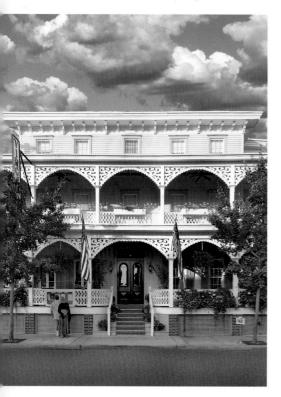

Other amenities include valet parking on weekends and in peak season, evening turndown service, and a complimentary continental breakfast complete with morning newspaper. During the summer, free beach chairs, towels, and umbrellas are available.

Adding to the hotel's appeal is its restaurant, the award-winning Ebbitt Room. One of the top restaurants in Cape May for fine dining, the Ebbitt Room adds to the Virginia's reputation as one of the town's premier destination locations.

The Virginia is typical of Cape May's finer Victorian hotels, which feature grace, charisma, and polished-wood charm over the sterility of the modern chain hotel. The Virginia's entrance is

The Virginia Hotel has retained its Victorian flavor. VIRGINIA HOTEL

Visiting the Virginia Hotel

25 Jackson St., Cape May, NJ 08204
Telephone: 609-884-5700 • Website: www.virginiahotel.com
E-mail: virginia@virginiahotel.com

Season: Open year-round.
Rooms: 24 guest rooms.
Handicap access: No.
Parking: On-street.
Credit cards: Accepted.
Personal checks: Accepted for deposit only.

right on the street, and to enter, you climb up a few wooden steps. Even the front desk is all polished wood and polite smiles.

Inside, the elegance and class of the Virginia quickly makes you realize you're in a special place. Piano music drifts from a nearby room. You hear the faint sounds of clinking dinnerware emanating from the Ebbitt Room, with its columned splendor and white-tablecloth sophistication. The sleekly polished wood is full of Old World charm but also sends a modern invitation to relax. The corridor, thick with its fine carpet, is full of guests coming and going, all enjoying the unique ambiance and savoring the fact that for the length of their stay, they're back in an era when a hotel stay meant more than just a heavy metal door with a peephole. And now you're back in that era too.

Eric notes that guests at the Virginia come from all over the world, especially Europe. That's no surprise. The Virginia is the one Victorian hotel in Cape May that is reminiscent of the finest hotels on the Continent.

Top right: The recently renovated Virginia Hotel is bright and airy. *Bottom right:* The Virginia Hotel's porch is a good spot to sit and enjoy a drink. VIRGINIA HOTEL

Food

Dining in Cape May is one of the greatest pleasures of a trip to the city. There are so many good restaurants in Cape May and the surrounding areas that you'll be hard-pressed to visit them all. Seafood, fine dining, American, Italian—virtually any type of cuisine you could desire is available in Cape May. It's no wonder the town is known as the restaurant capital of New Jersey.

Many folks find a favorite or two, then steadily expand outward, trying new establishments according to whim or recommendation. The nice thing is that it's rare to come up with a clunker in Cape May. Many restaurants are excellent for families and offer children's menus and other amenities.

At the height of a season or during a special event, restaurants may be crowded, and reservations at these times are strongly recommended. Most restaurants will not accept personal checks. As the hostess at one popular restaurant said, "What's a personal check?" New Jersey's no-smoking law prohibits smoking in any restaurant. If you want to smoke, you're going to have to go outside.

Food and drink are major parts of Cape May's appeal. CONGRESS HALL

EBBITT ROOM

The Ebbitt Room at the boutique Virginia Hotel is one of Cape May's most sophisticated and classiest restaurant. Everything about this superb establishment, from the white linen tablecloths to the unbelievable menu, is first-class all the way. The Ebbitt Room makes a special night spectacular.

The room gets its name from Alfred and Ellen Ebbitt, who built the Virginia Hotel in 1879. After serving for almost a century as a hotel, the entire structure was condemned in the early 1980s. Completely renovated, it reopened in 1989. Since then, the Ebbitt Room has set the standard for Cape May elegance.

The restaurant is located on the first floor of the Virginia Hotel. Use the

The Virginia Hotel's Ebbitt Room is a highly rated restaurant. VIRGINIA HOTEL

entrance for the hotel to access the restaurant. Understand that this is a pure gourmet restaurant, with selections that can't be found many other places. It's perfect for an intimate evening or a group of adults, but if somebody in your group eats only chicken nuggets or hot dogs, this isn't the place to go.

The main dining room is intimate without being claustrophobic. It seats about seventy. Even here you can hear the tinkling piano of popular local favorite Steve LaManna from the fireplace lounge. The Richmond Room seats another eighteen, and the outside terrace about fifteen. The subdued lighting adds to the overall effect.

Visiting the Ebbitt Room

Virginia Hotel, 25 Jackson St., Cape May, NJ 08204
Telephone: 609-884-5700 or 800-732-4236
Website: www.virginiahotel.com
E-mail: Ebbittroom@virginiahotel.com

Menu: Gourmet.
Attire: Casually elegant.
Hours: Dinner only, 5:30 to 10 P.M.
Handicap access: No.
Parking: Valet parking in-season.
Credit cards: Accepted.
Reservations: Accepted.

The Ebbitt Room has garnered so many awards that it would take several pages to list them all. It has a small but well-stocked bar. Appetizers include Seared Foie Gras, Tempura Calamari, and Duck Confit. Some of its superb entrees include Pan-Roasted Scottish Salmon, Pistachio-Dusted Scallops, and Roasted Rack of Lamb. The presentation on the plate is, as is everything else here, superb. By the way, if you don't try the homemade ice cream, your taste buds will hate you forever.

In season, there is valet parking—a feature not to be overlooked, as the alternative is the Great Parking Meter Hunt. As you can imagine, reservations are strongly recommended.

BLUE PIG TAVERN

Sure, it's named after an animal that isn't too particular about where it goes to dine, but don't let that fool you. The Blue Pig is one of Cape May's best restaurants.

The Blue Pig is located in the corner of Congress Hall nearest Perry Street. The restaurant has perhaps the oldest pedigree of any in Cape May. Back in the 1700s, a man named Elias Hughes operated a tavern for whalers here. It was the first of its kind to appear in the Cape May area. The eatery's distinctive name comes from a gambling parlor that used to be in Congress Hall in the 1850s.

The Blue Pig is cozy and comfortable, with a touch of whimsy. The restaurant offers several different dining areas. In nice weather, it's hard to beat a seat on the outdoor patio, lingering over coffee and the eatery's signature Benedict—a cheddar scallion biscuit with imported pancetta, poached eggs, and white truffle hollandaise—as you watch people stroll by on their way to the nearby beach or the

The Blue Pig at Congress Hall offers alfresco dining. CONGRESS HALL

Visiting the Blue Pig

Congress Hall, 251 Beach Ave., Cape May, NJ 08204
Telephone: 888-944-1816
E-mail: congress@congresshall.com
Website: www.congresshall.com

Menu: American.
Attire: Daytime casual, evenings dress casual.
Hours: Breakfast: Monday through Friday 7:30 to 11 A.M., Saturday 7:30 A.M. to 4 P.M., Sunday 7:30 A.M. to 3 P.M. Lunch: Sunday through Friday noon to 3 P.M., Saturday noon to 4 P.M. Dinner: Sunday through Thursday 5:30 to 9 P.M., Friday and Saturday 5:30 to 10 P.M.
Handicap access: Yes.
Parking: Private.
Credit cards: All major credit cards accepted.
Reservations: Accepted.

pedestrian mall. The terrace closes around the end of October. Inside, one dining room resembles an old-time tavern with a roaring fireplace and hardwood floors. The other inside dining area has a skylight that adds to the room's open, airy feeling. The inside dining rooms are big but still provide a "cozy private" feeling.

But it's the food that draws folks to the Blue Pig. The breakfast menu offers such things as eggs, pancakes, cereal, and fruit. Lunchtime features a wide variety, including burgers, Smoked Chicken and Brie, and Cornmeal-Dusted Catfish. Dinner selections include Pan-Seared Grouper Fillet, Steak Diane, and Rack of Lamb Dijon. The Blue Pig is particularly known for its pork chops and clam chowder.

The restaurant also wins points with families by featuring a different Blue Plate Special every day, such as spaghetti and meatballs on Tuesday, fillet of beef on Thursday, and roast pork shoulder on Sunday.

On the winter holidays—Thanksgiving, Christmas, and New Year's Eve—the Blue Pig offers special menus. During the Christmas season, the tavern dining room features an amusing Christmas tree decorated with silverware and—what else?—stuffed blue pigs.

HENRY'S ON THE BEACH

It's hard not to ignore the food at Henry's on the Beach and stare out at the beautiful ocean rolling in and out. Hard, that is, but not impossible, since the food at Henry's is so good. Sooner or later, you're going to exclaim, "Darn, that's good!" and tear your eyes off the ocean to look down at your plate. Then you'll notice that your kids are eating too. And not complaining. Miracle of miracles.

That's the kind of place Henry's is—a family restaurant on the beachfront that features both good food and a fantastic view. As far as the scenery, Henry's is completely open-air, so you can even smell that tangy sea spray. Many of the 200-capacity

Visiting Henry's on the Beach

702 Beach Dr., Cape May, NJ 08204
Telephone: 609-884-8826
Website: www.henrysonthebeach.com

Menu: American.
Attire: Casual.
Hours: Lunch: 11:30 A.M. to 3 P.M.
Dinner: 4:30 to 9:30 P.M.
Handicap access: Yes.
Parking: On-street.
Credit cards: All major credit cards accepted.
Reservations: Not accepted.
Children's menu: Yes.

restaurant's seats offer a great view of the beach and the water beyond. The restaurant is also handicap accessible.

Henry's is located on the Promenade, just a stone's throw from Convention Hall. Although some tables are under a roof, many in the back portion of the restaurant are not sheltered. The back of the building butts up against the beach, with the ocean shimmering just beyond. Getting there as dusk's long shadows begin to steal over the sand is something very special.

The atmosphere at Henry's is casual and relaxed. Kids bounce up and down in their seats. The restaurant gives them crayons and paper and lets them hang up the pictures they draw on a special wall. That just adds to the family-friendly atmosphere at Henry's, which the owners work hard at maintaining. As owner Ed Henry says, it's the kind of place in which he and his wife like to dine.

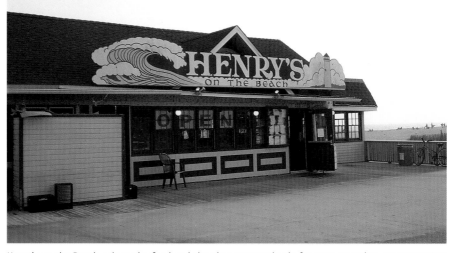

Henry's on the Beach, where the food and the view constantly vie for your attention. PAT KING-ROBERTS

Henry's is also family-friendly foodwise, in more ways than one. Most entrees are under $19.95, and there's a kids' selection of $6.95 dinners. Ed says that he doesn't like to be unpleasantly surprised at the prices when he goes out to eat, and he doesn't want his guests to be either.

The highlight of the menu is Chicken Mascarpone, a chicken breast stuffed with cheeses and seafood, and definitely not for the faint of appetite. The menu also features enough variety, with meat, seafood, Italian entrees, and a selection of sandwiches, that everyone's sure to find something he or she likes. An added bonus is that the restaurant features wine from the Cape May Winery.

The only drawback to Henry's is that, because of its location, it closes relatively quickly after the summer season is over. But while warm weather reigns, so does Henry's.

BELLA VÍDA GARDEN CAFÉ

Bella Vída (*bella* means "beautiful" in Italian, *vída* is slang for "life" in Costa Rica) used to be one of Cape May's best-kept secrets. But the cat's out of the bag now. Great foods, a varied menu, vegetarian-friendly, free parking . . . no wonder locals didn't want word to get out about this homey, affordable, family café in West Cape May.

The café's menu features salads and sandwiches, wraps, seafood, melts, Bella Burgers, triple-deckers, seafood, daily vegetarian specials, and more. Breakfast, which is served all day, is highlighted by Bella Vída's selection of specialty omelets, such as Mario's Marvel, with onions, peppers, hot sausage, and cheese. The salads are a menu highlight, including the Hallelujah Salad, with romaine lettuce, tomato, carrots, squash, raisins, red onion, cucumber, broccoli, and flaxseeds and sunflower seeds. Prices are reasonable, and the café's family-friendly atmosphere, with coloring books and crayons provided for the kids, is perfect for parents who don't want to constantly shush their children.

Visiting Bella Vída

406 N. Broadway, West Cape May, NJ 08204
Telephone: 609-884-6332
Website: www.bellavidacafe.com

Menu: American.
Attire: Casual.
Hours: Breakfast and lunch: Sunday 7 A.M. to 2:30 P.M., Monday through Saturday 7 A.M. to 3:30 P.M. Dinner: Tuesday through Saturday from 5 P.M.
Handicap access: No.
Parking: On-site.
Credit cards: Visa, MasterCard, and Discover.
Reservations: No.
Children's menu: Yes.

One of the best deals in Cape May is Bella Vída's 222, a breakfast special featuring two eggs, two pancakes, and two pieces of bacon for $2.22. It's only for weekday early birds–you have to be seated by 8 A.M. Monday through Friday–but your stomach and wallet will thank you.

There's a lot on the side of the restaurant for parking. The little yellow building is not much to look at–more house than business–but don't let that put you off. Locals have been eating at this place since the early 1900s. So pull up a chair at Bella Vída's and join a long-standing tradition.

MAD BATTER

Located on historic Jackson Street on the bottom floor of the Carroll Villa Hotel, the Mad Batter is a restaurant with a national reputation. It's a place simply not to be missed while you're in Cape May.

The Mad Batter is practically synonymous with Cape May. The restaurant participates in many MAC-sponsored activities and is known far and wide for its different events, and many Cape May happenings begin or end here.

You know you're in for something unusual the moment you walk in and see the wild, bright colors and the local artwork that decorates the walls. The Mad Batter is as quirky as its food is delicious. On the back wall, for example, is a large drawing of a tree. Sticking out from the wall is a lantern that looks like a beehive, giving the tree a three-dimensional appearance.

The Batter's skylit main dining room is deceptively large and unbelievably friendly. In warmer weather, you can dine right on the front porch, underneath a yellow-striped canopy that's a well-known image in Cape May. The restaurant is warm and friendly. Kids don't have to worry about being quiet, and parents don't have to worry about making them so.

Mad Batter breakfasts are legendary. Thick-sliced orange and almond French toast, oatmeal pancakes, and Irish oatmeal served with brown sugar and raisins

Visiting the Mad Batter

19 Jackson St., Cape May, NJ 08204
Telephone: 609-884-5970 • Website: www.madbatter.com
E-mail: mbatter@eticomm.net

Menu: American regional.
Attire: Casual.
Hours: Breakfast and lunch: 8 A.M. to 3 P.M. Dinner from 5 P.M.
Handicap access: Call for accommodation.
Parking: On-street.
Credit cards: Visa, MasterCard, American Express, and Discover.
Reservations: Accepted for dinner; not needed for breakfast or lunch.
Children's menu: Yes.

help you get your morning off to a good start. If you let your Cape May vacation get by without trying one of the Batter's signature egg dishes, such as Chesapeake Bay Benedict—poached eggs on a toasted English Muffin with jumbo lump crabmeat and caper hollandaise—you have only yourself to blame. When you enjoy all this delicious food on the front porch, there's no better way to start a Cape May day.

The lunch menu features soups and salads, super sandwiches, wraps, burgers, and more. The Pear Walnut Salad—romaine and radicchio tossed in walnut dressing with pears, Gorgonzola cheese, and toasted walnuts—is delightfully different and wonderfully delicious. For dinner, the Batter offers such entrees as Horseradish-Crusted Filet Mignon, Orange-Lavender-Roasted Chicken, Stuffed Figs with Gorgonzola Cheese, Crabmeat Cavatelli, and Chicken Satay, sweet and spicy seasoned strips of chicken breast with oriental-style peanut sauce. The Batter's Maryland Crab Cakes, served with sweet potato hash and mustard sauce, are perhaps the best on the planet. An excellent selection of microbrews is also available.

The Mad Batter's distinctive front sign, with the image of an *Alice in Wonderland*-type character, has been welcoming people to Cape May for a long time. Don't miss the opportunity to be one of them.

UGLY MUG

The Ugly Mug is for anybody who yearns for that classic pub look and feel. One of Cape May's oldest pubs, the Ugly Mug has a forest of mugs hanging from the ceiling that belonged to or currently belong to the Ugly Mug Club. If the mug faces east, the club member is deceased. If it faces west, he or she is alive and kicking—and probably due to have a belt at the Ugly Mug soon.

The Ugly Mug consists of a bar and a small dining room located on the Washington Street Mall. In nice weather, patrons can sit outside. This is pure pub food—burgers, fries, and sandwiches—but darn good. During lunch and dinner hours, the

Visiting the Ugly Mug

426 Washington Street Mall, Cape May, NJ 08204
Telephone: 609-884-3459
Website: www.uglymugenterprises.com

Menu: American and seafood.
Attire: Casual.
Hours: Lunch and dinner: 11 A.M. to 11 P.M.
Handicap access: Yes.
Parking: On-street.
Credit cards: Discover, MasterCard, Visa, and American Express.
Personal checks: Not accepted.
Reservations: Not accepted.
Children's menu: Yes.

Ugly Mug is a family dining place, with tables for parties of four or so and a children's menu. After 10 P.M., the Mug becomes more of a traditional bar.

The Ugly Mug offers lunch and dinner, and both are excellent because they come from the same menu. For twists on traditional dining, try the Cape Island Crab Patty, an Ugly Mug combination, or the Hot Ugly Sandwiches, or the Ocean Burger, a burger dripping with shrimp salad and sharp cheddar cheese. You can also get steak sandwiches that make you feel as if you're in Philadelphia, giant half-pound burgers, and Ugly Mug Platters.

Some people might argue that there are better places to bring the family than a pub. But the food is good, the prices are reasonable, and the servers are friendly, so don't be afraid that you're committing a parental faux pas if you bring the kids during eating hours. Just be warned, they'll probably bug you to death for an Ugly Mug T-shirt from the gift shop. Heck, you'll probably want one yourself.

CARRIAGE HOUSE TEAROOM AND CAFÉ

No Cape May Victorian experience is complete without lunch at the Carriage House Tearoom and Café. Located at the rear of the Carriage House on the Emlen Physick Estate (the building on the left of the driveway when you enter the estate grounds) and run by the Mid-Atlantic Center for the Arts (MAC), the tearoom offers several ways to immerse yourself in the Victorian way of life.

Tea at the Carriage House is the epitome of the Victorian experience. MID-ATLANTIC CENTER FOR THE ARTS

Visiting the Carriage House Tearoom and Café

Emlen Physick Estate, 1048 Washington St., Cape May, NJ 08204
Telephone: 609-884-5405, ext. 138
Website: www.capemaymac.org

Menu: Tea luncheon.
Attire: Casual.
Hours: Lunch: 11:30 A.M. to 2 P.M.
Elegant afternoon tea: 2 to 3 P.M.
Handicap access: Yes.
Parking: On-site.
Credit cards: Visa and MasterCard.
Reservations: Recommended.

First of all is the food. Mostly this is pure tearoom-type food—finger sandwiches, salads, soups, pastries, breads, scones, and selections like Smoked Turkey with Roasted Asparagus and Truffle Mayonnaise. In 2006, however, the menu was expanded to include other items such as wraps. The resident chef is excellent, serving up incredibly good food that is attractively presented. It's a gourmet's lunch or afternoon repast at its finest. This is lunch just like the Victorians did it.

The meal is served with a choice of any of a dizzying number of the distinctive Twinings teas. There are selections here that you can't find in your typical supermarket aisle. Indeed, the hardest choice you may have to make is not what to eat, but what to drink! Also be sure to order one of the scrumptious desserts, which are wonderfully decadent.

Although there are a few tables inside, the majority of the tearoom's tables are under a gigantic plastic four-sided canopy. A portable fireplace chases away the chill until the really cold weather arrives, after which time the canopy is taken down until it gets warm again. Normally the canopy stays up until after the Christmas holiday season, unless the weather is unusually severe. Parking for the restaurant is in the same large lot as for the Emlen Physick Estate.

Although the setting doesn't allow for much ambience in the way of plants, pictures, and so on, you won't notice or care because the food is so good. Besides, you'll find all the ambience you need in the adjoining shop.

Another way to experience the Victorian era is for ladies to choose from an ever-widening selection of Victorian hats to wear while enjoying lunch. The hats hang on the wall, and whichever one captures your fancy is yours for the wearing during your meal. This popular activity lends the perfect air of authenticity to the tearoom.

The Tearoom also offers elegant afternoon teas, beginning at 2 P.M. and featuring a sampling of tea breads, scones, sandwiches, and desserts. The tearoom does not serve breakfast or dinner.

Great food, an unusual setting, and Victorian hats to boot. What's more Cape May than that?

UNCLE BILL'S PANCAKE HOUSE

Uncle Bill's Pancake House is a great place to take the entire family. The food is great, it's reasonably priced, it's close to the beach . . . it's just too bad it doesn't do dinner.

Uncle Bill's was originally built in the 1950s as Congress Hall's beachfront cocktail bar. It's a good idea now, but back then Cape May would have none of it. Today Uncle Bill's serves breakfast and lunch, but breakfast is so delicious and filling that lunch can sometimes be an afterthought. More's the pity, since the menu of burgers, hot dogs, cheesesteaks, and other tasty sandwiches is perfect for a Cape May afternoon.

But it's breakfast that's the star here, and it's likely that Uncle Bill's hasn't ever gotten a bad review. As the name suggests, pancakes are here, in all their numerous varieties with various toppings, but you'll also find waffles, thick French toast slices, Hawaiian ham steaks, creamed chipped beef, and pigs in a blanket. Customer favorites include Uncle Bill's Special, a New York steak with eggs of your choice and pancakes, and Tiffany's Delight, a toasted English muffin with ham, eggs, and cheese.

With its unique circular shape, blue roof, and prominent corner position, you can't miss Uncle Bill's if you head along Beach Drive toward Congress Hall. Besides the good food and easy access, the restaurant also offers plenty of free parking.

In summer, you can usually arrive with a large party—say eight or so—without a reservation and still get seated together at one table. The restaurant is closed during January and February.

Uncle Bill's is the kind of relative you like to visit!

Visiting Uncle Bill's Pancake House

261 Beach Dr. (in front of Congress Hall), Cape May, NJ 08204
Telephone: 609-884-7199

Menu: American.
Attire: Casual.
Hours: Breakfast and lunch: 7 A.M. to 2 P.M.
Handicap access: Yes.
Parking: Off-street.
Credit cards: Not accepted.
Reservations: Not accepted.

YESTERDAY'S HEROES BALLPARK CAFÉ

If anyone in your party is a baseball fan, you absolutely have to go to Yesterday's Heroes Ballpark Café. Even if no one is, you should still bring the whole family here for a fun time and good, reasonably priced food.

You immediately know that you're in an interesting place when you walk in the front door and are greeted by Babe Ruth. This amazing animatronic figure, just like those at Disneyland, periodically talks and gestures. He fascinates children, and it's almost impossible to keep them sitting at the table when this figure is talking and moving.

Just so you don't forget the theme of the restaurant—baseball—even the tables have baseball designs on them. Then there's the baseball memorabilia, which is in every nook of the café, hanging on the walls or tucked away behind glass cases. There are seats, bats, gloves, trading cards, uniforms, autographs, photos, advertisements, balls . . . almost everything you could ever find at a major league baseball game except grass. The place is like a mini-Cooperstown (the town where the Baseball Hall of Fame is located), and that's no exaggeration. It would probably take the average fan a good two hours to view all the items. The hard-core fan could spend an entire day here. The owner says the café contains one of the largest collections of Babe Ruth items on public display, and it would be impossible to argue with him. The collection is advertised as being valued at over $1 million.

After spending some time looking at all these things, you'll eventually get hungry, and happily the Ballpark Café hits a home run in that department. The food here is good and reasonably priced. The menu items are named for former ballplayers, such as the Johnny Callison Club, the Moe Berger, and Dick Allen's Pulled Pork. The salads are fresh, and the appetizers, such as cheese sticks, buffalo shrimp, and chicken tenders, are delicious. The café also offers a mouthwatering selection of gourmet pizzas.

Come for the memorabilia and stay for the food. Or come for the food and stay for the memorabilia. Ah heck, just come. You can't strike out here.

Visiting Yesterday's Heroes Ballpark Café

1035 Beach Dr. (in front of Atlas Inn), Cape May, NJ 08204
Telephone: 609-884-7000, ext. 4 • Website: www.yesterdaysheroes.net
E-mail: info@yesterdaysheroes.net

Menu: American.
Attire: Casual.
Hours: Breakfast: 6 to 11 A.M. Lunch: 11 A.M. to 3 P.M.
Dinner: 5 P.M. to 11 P.M.
Handicap access: Yes.
Parking: On-site.
Credit cards: Accepted.
Reservations: Accepted.
Children's menu: Yes.

WASHINGTON INN

With its distinctive long, red canopy stretching from its front door all the way to the Washington Street sidewalk, the Washington Inn announces that it's someplace special, and it surely is. This is the founding father of fine dining in Cape May, the one that blazed the trail for all the great restaurants that have since followed. When the inn first opened, Cape May was still evolving as a Victorian resort town. The Washington Inn quickly became *the* place to eat in town. Other fine restaurants moved in, and today you can't throw a pebble without hitting a top-quality eatery.

The restaurant is just down the street from the Emlen Physick Estate, in the direction of the pedestrian shopping mall. Built in 1840 as a plantation house, the Washington Inn is another Cape May restaurant that contains multiple dining rooms, each much different from the other. One is an intimate dining room with a fireplace, and another has a display of greenery and plants on the far wall.

Although it may look like just another restaurant from the outside, there's something intimate and warm about the Washington Inn. It has been called one of the top places in New Jersey to get married. It has an air of romance about it, certainly, but it also has an atmosphere of friendliness and warmth that makes it special.

The Washington Inn changes its menu multiple times throughout the year. It features primarily an American cuisine, with such selections as Pan-Seared Filet Mignon and Rack of Lamb. The inn's desserts are famous throughout Cape May and beyond. Although it may be tough, you owe it to yourself—and your taste

The Washington Inn's distinctive red canopy is a Cape May landmark. PAT KING-ROBERTS

Visiting the Washington Inn

801 Washington St., Cape May, NJ 08204
Telephone: 609-884-5697 • Website: www.washingtoninn.com
E-mail: washinn@bellatlantic.net

Menu: American/Italian
Attire: Dressy casual.
Hours: 5 to 10 P.M.
Handicap access: Yes.
Parking: On-street.
Credit cards: All major credit cards accepted.
Reservations: Accepted.

---

buds—to try one. In addition, the restaurant has the most extensive wine cellar in southern New Jersey, stocked with more than 500 bottles.

The Washington Inn has published a cookbook called *Washington Inn Cooks for Friends*, with 350 of the restaurant's favorite recipes.

FAST FOOD

We all get a craving for fast food now and then. If you have kids, they get the craving every thirty-eight seconds or so. This McDonald's is the only fast-food chain restaurant within spitting distance of Cape May. Cape May proper and West Cape May do not have any.

To get here from Cape May, follow the signs for the Cape May–Lewes Ferry. When you see the shopping center with the Acme on your right, you're almost there. McDonald's will be visible from the right. Take a right turn at the next light, and you're there.

McDonald's
Bayshore Rd. and Sandman Blvd.
North Cape May, NJ 08204
Telephone: 609-884-0840

ICE CREAM

Ben and Jerry's ice cream. Need more be said?

Ben and Jerry's Scoop Shop
414 Washington St. (on the pedestrian mall)
Cape May, NJ 08204
Telephone: 609-884-3040

ACKNOWLEDGMENTS

Despite what you always see on television and in the movies, books, especially nonfiction, are rarely written by a solitary figure locked away in some small room pounding away on a typewriter or keyboard. Books are a collaborative effort among many people. This volume owes a debt to Jenn Heinold, Jean Barraclough, Kyle Weaver, and all the folks in Cape May who put up with me.

The book is dedicated to all those teachers who realized that my math ineptitude was staggering and pointed me toward a career using the English language so that I wouldn't spend the rest of my life operating a music box with a trained monkey. And as always, special thanks go to Patti for her support and help. I couldn't have done it without her.

INDEX